OUDTESTAMENTISCHE STUDIËN

DEEL XIX

OUDTESTAMENTISCHE STUDIËN

NAMENS HET OUDTESTAMENTISCH
WERKGEZELSCHAP IN NEDERLAND

UITGEGEVEN DOOR

A. S. VAN DER WOUDE
GRONINGEN

DEEL XIX

LEIDEN
E. J. BRILL
1974

LANGUAGE AND MEANING

STUDIES IN HEBREW LANGUAGE AND BIBLICAL EXEGESIS

PAPERS READ AT THE
JOINT BRITISH-DUTCH OLD TESTAMENT CONFERENCE
HELD AT LONDON, 1973

BY

J. BARR, W. A. M. BEUKEN, A. GELSTON,
J. C. L. GIBSON, C. J. LABUSCHAGNE,
C. VAN LEEUWEN, L. R. WICKHAM

LEIDEN
E. J. BRILL
1974

This volume contains the papers read at the Joint British Dutch Old Testament conference held at King's College, Halliday Hall, 67 South Side, Clapham Common, London from 3-6 January 1973.

On behalf of the Oudtestamentisch Werkgezelschap in Nederland *the editor of* Oudtestamentische Studiën *likes to express warmest thanks to the British Society for Old Testament Study for its hospitality and friendship* : הנה מה־טוב ומה־נעים שבת אחים גם־יחד

ISBN 90 04 039430

PRINTED IN BELGIUM

INHOUD

ETYMOLOGY AND THE OLD TESTAMENT [1]

BY

JAMES BARR

Manchester

In recent years the value of etymology for biblical interpretation has fallen into some considerable uncertainty, and for this uncertainty the present writer must bear some responsibility. In my book on *The Semantics of Biblical Language* I made some strong criticisms of the use of etymology in the word-studies then popular. I nowhere said that etymology was without value as a form of study or without interest as a mental exercise; but I did deny that it was a guide to the meaning of words in the contexts in which they are used. Thus for instance I argued [2]:

> It must be emphasized that this is a historical study. It studies the past of a word, but understands that the past of a word is no infallible guide to its present meaning. Etymology is not, and does not profess to be, a guide to the semantic value of words in their current usage, and such value has to be determined from the current usage and not from derivation.

In the discussions which followed the publication of *Semantics* my criticisms of the over-use of etymology were, I believe, very widely accepted, and it was readily accorded that the practice of etymologizing had led to some quite outrageous misinterpretation of biblical locutions. Nevertheless it continued to be felt that etymology must somehow have *some* value for the understanding of biblical language, and I myself had granted this. If etymological study, then, is not to be totally rejected, we should try to say something more precise about its value and demarcate more exactly the line that separates its proper use from its misuse. We may begin, then, by summarizing three general

---

[1]) The present article gives a summary of the writer's thoughts about this subject, and omits many aspects; it is hoped to publish a fuller survey later.

[2]) *Semantics*, p. 107.

reasons which appear to favour the continuing importance of etymology:

a. It is not in dispute that etymology is in principle a valid form of study and that it can furnish valuable insights into the history and the background of words.

b. Etymology is particularly important for the identification and elucidation of rare words and *hapax legomena*. The Hebrew Bible has many such rare words, and these can often be elucidated only through comparison with words in Ugaritic, Akkadian, Arabic and other cognate languages; this was expressly admitted by me in *Semantics*[1]).

c. Etymology is not something confined to the modern world. On the contrary, the etymological consciousness was already very strong in the ancient world, and notably so in the milieu of the Bible, of early Judaism and of early Christianity. If, then, the men of biblical times already thought etymologically and had an interest in the etymological interpretation of their own language, then we today, if we should discount etymology, are in danger of ignoring something that was a real and important part of their thinking, and thus in danger of misunderstanding the way in which language actually functioned in their society (c.f. e.g. E. JACOB, *Théologie de l'A.T.*[2], Neuchatel 1968, p. v).

Are there then two sides to etymology, one good and the other bad? Or is there some confusion in the discussion, some misunderstanding of the terms of it? In this paper I propose to clarify this apparent uncertainty through an analysis of the concept of ctymology, as it is used in biblical study. I hope to show that there is no single thing that is etymology; what we call by this name is not one process but several. We use it, in relation to biblical language study and exegesis, for a variety of different linguistic operations, which may have rather little to do with one another. When we realize that these operations are in fact different, and that arguments valid for one of them cannot be simply transferred to another, then some of the uncertainty which has been mentioned may perhaps be removed.

---

1) *Semantics*, p. 158. This passage was cited by D. HILL, *Greek Words and Hebrew Meanings* (Cambridge 1967), p. 4, n. 1, with the purpose of showing that I too must agree that "no reasonable person will wish to maintain that the original or etymological meaning of a word (when it is discoverable) cannot, in any circumstances, assist our understanding of its present semantic value". For my general reactions to HILL's arguments see my "Common Sense and Biblical Language" in *Biblica* xlix (1968), pp. 377-87. Cf. also G. FRIEDRICH, "Semasiologie und Lexikologie", *ThLZ* xciv (1969), col. 801-16, who (col. 811) takes up the same point and supposes it to be a contradiction in my position.

It follows from this that I do not propose to begin with a "correct" definition of etymology; rather, we begin from what people, perhaps confusedly, are in the habit of calling by this name, often without too much exactitude or too much nicety of discrimination. Taking the totality of what is thus customarily referred to as "etymology", I think that we shall find it a diversified ragbag of operations, such that no single definition would fit. Or, to put it in another way, if "etymology" were to be given a rigorous definition, the result would be to exclude some of the processes still generally had in mind by those who use the term.

It will be convenient if we begin by separating off two major types of operation, one of which we shall call scholarly etymology and the other popular etymology. Our subject in the first place will be scholarly etymology, and we shall return to popular etymology only at a later stage. This is not because popular etymology lacks importance; on the contrary, it has very great importance in the functioning of language. But we are talking in the first place about etymology as a discipline which trained scholars and exegetes are willing to use and to accept as a valid scholarly exercise.

We shall state therefore some characteristics which appear to be essential to modern scholarly etymology. The foundation of this discipline, we may say, was laid in the nineteenth century, and the following elements were basic to that foundation:

a. A historical perspective, the perception of a chronological development which forms the scale against which linguistic change is traced.

b. A classification of languages, by which it is known which languages are cognate with others, which may have had an historical influence upon others, and so on.

c. A satisfactory series of phonological correspondences between different languages, or between different stages of the same language. Where this element of phonological correspondence is not strictly observed, etymology becomes a mere loose association between words that look alike or sound alike and that have some sort of imaginable association of meaning; and such indeed was the state of most etymological study before modern scholarly methods were worked out [1].

---

[1] Cf. recently L. R. PALMER, *Descriptive and Comparative Linguistics: a Critical Introduction* (London 1972), p. 300: "It was the discovery of the sound law principle that delivered etymology from dilettantism and from the reproach that etymology is a science in which the consonants count for very little and the vowels for nothing at all".

In popular etymology, unlike modern scholarly etymology, these essential elements are usually lacking : popular etymology has lacked a historical perspective; it has been confused about the relations between one language and another; and it has had no clear appreciation of the importance of sound correspondences in determining the relations between one word and another. The relations which it perceives, the assonances, similarities and associations, are occasional, accidental and non-universalizable; its perception of them is undisciplined. It is because scholarly etymology has a disciplined and regular procedure that it can produce imposing results, and it is the use of scholarly etymology that forms the centre of the problem of etymology in modern biblical study.

For the present therefore we concentrate on scholarly etymology, and within it I propose to distinguish several different operations, any of which is likely in its own way to be termed or to be deemed etymological. In other words, what we now offer is something like a typology of etymological study, as it may be exemplified in its application to the Old Testament and its linguistic milieu [1]).

Etymology A : prehistoric reconstruction

Our first type of etymological operation is the reconstruction of form and sense in a so-called proto-language — in our case, proto-Semitic or, as it may be, proto-North-West-Semitic, or proto-Indo-European, proto-Germanic, and so on. This proto-language *ex hypothesi* no longer exists; there are no texts in it, no examples in quotable form; one cannot cite its forms or their sense on the basis of hard direct evidence. By its own nature the proto-language lies anterior to express historical documentation. The basis, upon which all reconstructions of the proto-language are founded, lies within the historically-evidenced languages only. Thus for proto-Semitic all the hard evidence lies within the attested languages like Hebrew, Arabic, Akkadian, Ugaritic. From known forms with known senses in these languages, projections are made of the probable forms and senses in the ancestor language.

---

[1]) What I intend here, however, is something rather different from the scope of the article "A tentative Typology of Etymological Studies" by Yakov Malkiel, one of the chief modern connoisseurs of the theory and practice of etymology: see his *Essays on Linguistic Themes* (Oxford 1968), pp. 199-227. His article is rather a typology of the methods and views of professional etymologists; mine is rather a typology of the processes likely to be met with within biblical study.

A common mode of reconstruction is by means of a triangulation process, which may be illustrated from a familiar term like the Semitic words having the verb root *'-m-r*. In extant languages we have evidenced forms such as Hebrew *'amar* "say", Arabic *'amara* principally "command", Akkadian *amāru* "see", Ethiopic *ammără* "show". These acknowledged and quotable facts are taken as the base of the triangle, and the apex is supposed to represent a proto-Semitic sense. Thus, for instance, the recent Hebrew dictionary of BAUMGARTNER, recording this information from the various languages, then offers us a notice like this :

?Grdb. hell sein, sehen, sichtbar machen > kundtun

That is to say, it is a reasonable hypothesis that in the proto-language the sense was "be clear, see, make visible", and from this there developed a sense "make known" ; such a development, it is suggested, would provide an adequate explanation of the known senses in diverse Semitic languages, from which we started out. We could represent the operation diagrammatically thus :

Hebr. *'amar* "say" Arab. *'amara* "command" Eth. *ammără* "show; know" Akkad. *amāru* "see"	proto-Semitic sense "be clear" ?

I shall not discuss whether this particular reconstruction is satisfying or not; I cite it merely as an example of the sort of reconstruction that may quite commonly be made.

About this sort of etymology the following general points may be made. Firstly, all such reconstructions, and indeed all etymologies of any kind, involve two aspects, a phonological and a semantic. As we have seen, modern scholarly etymology depends on a set of phonological correspondences between cognate languages, and these in turn give access, at least in hypothetical form, to the phoneme stock of the ancestor language; tables, providing this information in concise form, are standard material of all comparative grammars. Alongside the phonological aspect there is a semantic aspect : the meanings in the historical languages may suggest what the meaning in the ancestor language may have been, and this in turn may suggest what was the semantic path, in our own case the semantic path from a pre-Hebrew stage to the evidenced meaning in biblical Hebrew. In the example cited, that of *'amar* and cognates, probably all would accept that the forms belong together on the phonological side; the task of semantic reconstruction, on the other hand, is materially harder in this case, and this is rightly acknowledged by Professor BAUMGARTNER with his question mark. In other cases, perhaps, the semantic associations may seem fairly obvious, and the real difficulty may lie on the phonological side, which may make it doubtful whether words, apparently of very like meaning, are really cognate: compare the familiar instances of English *have* and Latin *habēre*, English *day* and Latin *dies*, which look as if they were obviously related but which, we are told, by strict phonological criteria cannot be so.

The second point is this: in order to establish the validity and importance of this type of etymology, it is by no means necessary that one should be able to carry out a successful and complete reconstruction of form and sense in the proto-language. In spite of the increasing refinement of our methods, there are several reasons why we are no more likely to produce definitive accounts of the forms and meanings in proto-Semitic than was the case a century ago. But, though such reconstruction must remain in the realm of the hypothetical, even as hypothesis its function is very important: the "comparisons" that we carry out, i.e. the operations in which we align an Arabic or an Akkadian word with a Hebrew word, all imply that these languages and the words in question have a common prehistory. They are cognate in the sense of being descended from a common past; but for the assurance that some such common prehistory had existed, we would in many cases not be justified in carrying out any comparative operation at all.

I shall here add, without developing the matter, two ways in which Etymology A may make itself noticeable through its practical implications. Firstly, where homonyms have arisen through causes such as phoneme merger (e.g. proto-Semitic *'ayin* and *ghain*, according to general opinion, merged into *'ayin* in Hebrew), Etymology A is the process by which a distinction between words now homonymic may be established: in Hebrew, for instance, between *'ana* "answer" and *'ana* "sing", just as in English between the familiar word *ear* (cogn. Latin *auris*) and the other *ear* (of corn)(cogn. Latin *acus*). The practical importance of this sort of discrimination is obvious in the Hebrew dictionary. Secondly, Etymology A is used in attempts to reconstruct not a linguistic, but a non-linguistic history: to deduce, let us say, from elements which seem to be common to the entire language family something about the geographical area in which its speakers once dwelt, something about the culture which they then had in common. This sort of application of etymology is familiar from nineteenth-century researches. Both the above are applications of Etymology A.

Etymology B : historical tracing within an observable development

With this we pass to our Etymology B, which is the tracing of forms and meanings within an observable historical development. Thus in Greek we can trace the development of a word in sense and sound from Homer down to the New Testament, to the middle ages or to modern spoken Greek, and in English we can trace a word back, perhaps, to the earliest extant sources in Old English. In Hebrew we may be able to do the same and thus to trace words from early poems down to Sirach and the Mishnah, and indeed beyond into the middle ages and down to the usage of present-day Israel. If, in the case of Hebrew, we find ourselves unable to carry this out in full, it will very likely be not because of any difficulty in principle, but because of one simple difficulty, namely the lack of adequate information.

For our present purpose the main point to notice is the difference from the situation in our Etymology A. In case B the operation is less hypothetical and less reconstructive in character : it works within one known language and traces development through different stages, all of which are extant in historical documents. Thus within Hebrew, if we start from *minḥa* with the late sense "evening religious service", we might perhaps set out an etymology somewhat as follows :

minḥa { "evening service" / "cereal offering" } < "religious offering" to God) (in general) < ("gift"(to man or God)

All these stages could be documented from extant texts. Again, we are not concerned whether this is a correct tracing of the development or not; it is put forward simply as an example.

Some further points about Etymology B may be briefly made. First of all, within the Bible itself there may often be some uncertainty about the chronological sequence of sources, and some kind of historical source analysis may be required in order that this sort of etymological tracing should be carried out. This is, however, a difficulty in execution rather than one in principle : all of us are agreed that we can *sometimes* succeed in distinguishing between earlier and later sources within the Bible. In any case, as soon as we leave the special case of the biblical literature, we find it possible to construct some kind of historical scale for our documents for Sirach, let us say, or for the Qumran scrolls, for the Mishnah and the Talmud. In principle therefore the apparatus for a historical tracing of Hebrew etymology within type B is already present and is indeed taken for granted in general outline.

Secondly, we have seen that type B, in comparison with type A, is less hypothetical and reconstructive in character, in that it works not by comparative means, but within one developing language stream and from extant texts. But even so we must observe that an element of reconstruction is still present : though we may have stage one and stage two, both within Hebrew and in extant texts, the path from stage one to stage two is seldom known with absolute objectivity; some element of reconstructive imagination is necessary, and by consequence doubt can always be cast upon reconstructions of the historical process. Nobody, after all, has left us a written record of why or under what circumstances *minḥa* came to be used of an *evening* offering in particular, or of a *cereal* offering rather than any other kind; we can no doubt suggest very probable explanations, but the development of meaning is not described for us by the sources in black and white. Under these circumstances, how do we assess the probability of various explanations of changes of meaning? Basically, I would suggest, in two ways : firstly, by noting contemporary developments in thought and culture—in our example, let us say, the rise of systems of technical sacrificial terminology, codification of the priestly and Levitical laws, and so on; and, secondly, some sort of preliminary classification, based on our previous linguistic experience, of the ways in which meanings may be found to change and develop : let us suppose, by metonymy, by extension, by loss of a semantic element [1]). Thus, to summarize this point, though Etymology B, working from extant forms in extant texts, is less hypothetical and reconstructive in character than Etymology A, it still has a reconstructive character also.

Finally, some might question whether type B, as described, is really

---

[1]) Cf. the widely-recognized work of G. STERN, *Meaning and Change of Meaning. With special Reference to English* (Göteborgs Högskolas Årsskrift xxxviii, 1931), a patient and detailed analysis of the possibilities in this regard.

etymology. Is it not rather historical semasiology, or historical lexicography, or something of that order? Well, if this does not count as etymology, then we may simply subtract it from our list and ignore it. But my own observation suggests that, when biblical scholars or other people refer to the "etymology" of a word, some observations they have in mind belong in fact to our type B. I would not find it surprising, for instance, if I heard someone say that Latin *persona* "etymologically" meant "mask"; and any statement of this form would belong to my type B. But it is right, and important, to observe that historical semasiology, or historical lexicography, and Etymology B do not coincide. An interest in linguistic development, in meaning change and so on, is usually regarded as etymological only when it is an origin-seeking process, when its interest lies in the beginning of the development rather than in the subsequent stages. A historical tracing of development, if its interest was primarily in the later stages, would hardly be termed etymological. In this sense etymology is biassed towards the beginnings.

Etymology C: identification of adoptions from another language

Our third type concerns the identification and tracing back of so-called "loan-words". Thus, to give an easy example, it is common practice to say that Hebrew *hekal* "temple" is derived from the Akkadian *ekallu* and it in its turn from the Sumerian *e gal* "great house". Biblical Hebrew had a good number of such words but still not an enormous number; its proportion of such adoptions within the total vocabulary must have been very much lower than is the case in a modern language like English, which has an enormous number drawn from French, Latin and Greek, as well as other sources. In later Hebrew such adoptions became more frequent, sources such as Persian, Greek and Latin being drawn upon. The other great source, of course, is Aramaic, a result of the symbiosis of the two languages in Jewish culture over a considerable period.

In Etymology C the task is to identify that words are in fact adoptions, to identify the language from which they came, their meaning in that language and, if there is sufficient information, the date of their adoption into Hebrew. Behind this adoption there lies, of course, a further etymological history within their own language—as has already been briefly indicated for the familiar case of *hekal*. Naturally, the adoption of a word within Hebrew may have taken place a long time before the date of the earliest Hebrew text in which it appears. In these respects the case of *hekal*, which looks at first like a rather simple one, is in fact quite complex. In respect of date of adoption, the fact that it was used at Ugarit might seem to suggest that it was indigenized quite early in the Syrian-Canaanite language area. But against this must be set the statistics of usage in the Hebrew Bible, which indicate that *hekal*, though used in early sources, became common much later — it never appears in the Pentateuch or Joshua or Judges, and is rare in Samuel and the early prophets; it becomes common in the later prophets such as Jeremiah and Ezekiel (so already *BDB*, s.v.). Moreover, any discussion of the word in Hebrew must be diversified according to various semantic applications: its normal Akkadian usage seems to be of the royal palace rather than the temple of a deity, while in Hebrew the reverse is the case. Again, when used as a technical term in descriptions of the Solomonic temple, which is surely a basic case by any account and also is the place of many of the earlier occurrences, it is well known that the *hekal* is not what we would call the temple building but a particular section of it [1]). I do not intend to work this out here : I cite it merely as an instance of the complexities that may be involved in any assessment that a word is a loan-word, even where the information required is quite plentifully available.

Moreover, continuing with the case of *hekal*, and accepting that the derivation from Sumerian *e gal* with the sense of "great house" is correct, we should observe that this information, however true, is probably entirely irrelevant to the semantics of *hekal* in the Old Testament, since there is no evidence, and no likelihood, that any Hebrew speaker knew that the word came from Sumerian or what it meant in that language; nor does the sense in that language give a proper impression of its sense in Hebrew.

This leads me on to a general point aboute tymology and loan-words which may be not directly applicable to the biblical languages but is certainly important for people's general ideas about etymology and its value for semantic judgements. One can hardly doubt that one main reason for the importance that is popularly ascribed to etymological

---

[1]) There is evidence for Akkadian *ekallu* also as a part of a building, rather than the building as a whole. Incidentally, the time of adoption of loan-words may be indicated, if sufficient information exists, through the varying phonetic realizations in the new language of the sounds of the source language : in this case, the question whether Akkadian *k* is represented in Hebrew by *k* or by *g*.

perception as a form of linguistic expertise is the tremendous incidence of loan-words in modern languages like English and French—we may contrast the case of (say) the ancient Greeks, who knew comparatively little of foreign words within their own language, and whose own etymological excursions were almost entirely intra-Hellenic. Now, within words adopted from another language, it is important to distinguish between words taken over from another language along with the sense in which they are used in that language, and words formed from elements which do indeed have their origin in another language but have now become normal native elements in their own language. A good example is the common modern English word *technology*. People might commonly say that this word is "derived from the Greek" but this is true only in a restricted sense. *Technology* was formed not from Greek, nor on the basis of senses existing in Greek, but from the *English* (or other modern European) elements *techn-* (as in *technical*, and with that sense) and *-ology* (as in *geology*). These elements did indeed have their origin in Greek but this is not directly indicative of their function in modern English *technology*. There is indeed even an ancient (or strictly a Hellenistic) word τεχνολογία (and also τεχνόλογος): they mean a systematic treatment of grammar, and the writer of such works [1]). But this word has nothing to do with the formation of the English word *technology* and none of those who use the word know or care about the Greek one; the elements which form *technology* are elements which from the productive aspect have become operative units of English. Thus, in general, even in languages like English, the popular impression that a knowledge of the derivation is the obvious route to an understanding of words is confused and exaggerated. We need not, however, pursue this point farther, and something similar will emerge again shortly.

Etymology D: analysis of words into component morphemes

When the term "etymology" is used, it commonly designates a separation and identification of the constituent parts of words. In languages like English this is commonly connected with our long com-

[1]) The words are found in the *Rhetorica* of Philodemus (1st century B.C.); see Liddell and Scott, s.v.

pound words : the educated user of English is supposed to know that *misanthrope* comes from elements which (in Greek, for which aspect we revert to our Etymology C) mean "hate" and "mankind", and similarly that *odontology* includes as its first constituent the Greek word for "tooth". Knowledge of this kind of etymology is by no means necessary for the proper use of the language; hundreds of medical and scientific terms, for instance, like *odontology* are derived from Greek, but the doctors and scientists who use them perfectly well may generally know nothing of the form or of the sense of the Greek elements out of which they are formed—and quite justifiably, since by my previous argument these elements function in the words in question as *English,* not as *Greek,* lexical units.

The instance of Greek, however, may be followed up a little farther, since it may have something more to teach us about popular attitudes to etymology. Greek has of course many compound words, and in a case like λειτουργία "public service", later "religious service", it would be common practice to say that the word was "derived" from λαός "people" and ἔργον "work"; or, similarly, that ἐκκλησία "assembly, church" "comes from" ἐκ "out" and καλεῖν "call". As I pointed out in previous discussions [1]), such assessments ignore the word-formation in the compound, for the element λειτ- is not identical with λαός, the element -κλησία not identical with καλεῖν, etc. What commonly happens in fact is that people quote the *simplest* form, i.e. either the one which is most common and best known, or the one which in the grammatical tradition is the usual citation-form (in Greek, the nominative singular of nouns, the 1st person singular present or the infinitive of verbs, etc.; in Hebrew, in "western" grammar commonly the 3rd singular masculine perfect of verbs, except for some types like *qum,* cited by the "infinitive construct"; the indigenous Hebrew grammatical tradition, unlike the "western", generally cites by use of the "infinitive absolute" or else *l*^{e} plus the infinitive construct). What passes for etymology in many such cases is then the citation of the simpler, more familiar or more elementary form. This is connected with the aspiration to transparency, which as we shall shortly see is a main ingredient in the etymological consciousness.

For the present however we shall turn to the situation in Hebrew. Compound words of types like λειτουργία or *technology* are here uncom-

---

[1]) See *Semantics,* pp. 102, 111, 150, 165, 236, etc.; the two words cited are discussed in *Semantics,* but partly from other points of view.

mon or of slight importance, except for the special (but very important) case of personal names like Methuselah, Obadiah, etc. [1]). But Hebrew words can often perhaps be treated as *composita* in a different sense : many words can be regarded as formed out of two elements, a root morpheme and a pattern. Thus in the common *seper* "book" we say that the root morpheme is *s-p-r*, while the pattern is *-e-e-* ; with another pattern the same root morpheme forms *sipper* "he related", *mispar* "number", and so on. When people say that *mispar* is "derived" from the root *s-p-r*, this identification may also be called a sort of etymology. With this, however, we are once again moving to yet another type of operation. This is not a historical process : there never was a time when *s-p-r* existed before, or independently of, the words which include it. The relation of a Hebrew word to its root is not necessarily, and is commonly in fact not, a relation of historical derivation. This fact brings us to the interesting general reflection that *derivation* is an ambiguous term : it can refer to a historical process, working with categories of before and after; but it can also refer to a relationship which may rather be called generative [2]). It is interesting to recall that in some older grammars the term *etymology* was used for a section covering something like word-formation, rather than for a historical investigation [3]).

The common type of Semitic root like *s-p-r* does not appear independently but only in formed words, compounded with a pattern (the pattern being of vowels plus additional consonants, taken from a group which are used in patterns), and the relation between such a root and the formed word *seper* "book" is not a historical one but a generative one.

In such cases, in so far as etymology is the identification of the root, it is not a historical process. In complex cases both aspects may be present : if we take a modern Hebrew word like *makbesah* "laundry" [4]),

---

[1]) The explanation of *hekal* on the basis of Sumerian *e* plus *gal* (cf. above) can be regarded as another instance of the same kind of thing.

[2]) On this compare the careful article of R. C. DEARMOND, "The Concept of Word Derivation", *Lingua* xxii (1969), pp. 329-61, which itself expressly limits its scope to the "non-transformational" concept of derivation.

[3]) GESENIUS-KAUTZSCH-COWLEY gives "Etymology, or the Parts of Speech" as the title of the second, and indeed the major, part of Hebrew grammar; English edition, p.99.

[4]) The fact that the word is a modern one does not make it in any way inapt for illustration of our subject; the generative relation between roots and formed words in modern formations seems to me very similar to that which existed in ancient times; in any case examples from within biblical times could equally well be cited.

one can say that the relation of the root *k-b-s* to the full form is a generative one, the root being united with the pattern in question; but one can also say that there is a historical aspect, in as much as other formations from *k-b-s*, such as the piel verb *kibbes*, which is biblical, factually existed long before the noun formation *makbesah* was first formed [1]). An instance like *masoret* is complex in another way : modern dictionaries, or some of them, analyse it as having the root *'-s-r*; but even if this is historically right it is also likely that the word, understood in the sense "tradition", came to be analysed in the minds of speakers as having the root *m-s-r*, the common latish word meaning "to hand down, deliver" (tradition). If this were true, then we would have to treat the word as having the generative root *m-s-r* even if historically the earlier generative root had been *'-s-r*.

This brings us to the often discussed question whether or not it is helpful to speak about a meaning of the root or to speak only about the meanings of the words containing the root [2]). We may take the instance of the familiar root *š-l-m*. Extant formations include *šalom* (traditional gloss : "peace"), *šalem* ("entire, whole") and *šillem* ("pay"). I here ignore the more complex cases where there is a possibility of two or more homonymous roots. If one insisted on stating the meaning of the root *š-l-m* purely generatively and synchronically, one might in the end be doing no more than offering an addition or multiplication of the senses of the three words as we have them (unless one gave a sort of logical priority to one of the formations as against the others, which would seem to be biassed). It might be more meaningful to say this : that at some prehistorical point the root *š-l-m* (and words incorporating it) had such and such a meaning, but that in the course of time the three separate words had come to lie within distinct semantic fields, so that their relation to the common sense of the root was now purely a historical one and no useful synchronic statement of the root meaning was possible. To put this in another way, the achievement of a statement of the common meaning would belong to something like our

---

1) If it is correct that *k-b-s* "originally" meant "tread down", and so "wash clothes", I would consider this generatively irrelevant; it would belong to Etymology A and be valid in a prehistorical sense. In biblical and later Hebrew *k-b-s* is specialized for the washing of clothes and never means treading down in general; *k-b-š* is a different matter, for it never means "wash", and its development is in the quite other direction of "tread down, subdue, conquer".

2) On this, and on many points involved in this paper, see J. F. A. Sawyer, "Root-meanings in Hebrew", *JSS* xii (1967), pp. 37-50.

Etymology A or a modification of it (the base line being constituted not by words from other Semitic languages, or not necessarily so, but by a set of Hebrew words), while etymology D, working synchronically, could not produce a common meaning.

Thus I am now inclined to suggest that the question, whether a "root meaning" can usefully and meaningfully be stated for a Hebrew root or word group, will depend on the semantic history of the individual group of words concerned. Where words having a common root have also remained within the same semantic field, then there seems to be no good reason why a meaning for this root should not be assigned; but where they have not done so, then the semantic relationship between root and formed word may differ for each word and the relationship of the word meanings to the root meaning is definable only in historical terms. If this is so, then (contrary to tradition) all Hebrew words cannot be given a uniform treatment in this respect.

In any case, we conclude our survey of Etymology D by remarking that, if the identification of the root is accepted as a form of etymology, which would surely be generally granted, within Hebrew this will be a mixture of historical and non-historical processes, with the non-historical probably predominating. The historical emphasis of my earlier statement, cited at the beginning of this article, should now be modified in this respect.

Etymology E: use of a cognate language to discover the sense in Hebrew

We now come to the heuristic process through which the sense of obscure Hebrew words is elucidated by reference to words of apparently cognate form and of known meaning in other languages such as Ugaritic, Arabic and Akkadian. I have already studied this operation at length in my book *Comparative Philology and the Text of the Old Testament* and do not wish to elaborate upon it further. This approach depends in most cases upon the same sort of hypotheses as Etymology A, in other words it depends on the reconstruction of a prehistoric state; but the direction of the operation is different: in Etymology A the Hebrew sense functions, along with Arabic or Ugaritic or other cognates, as base evidence from which the prehistoric state can be projected; in Etymology E the Hebrew sense is the thing to be discovered. The word which stands in the Hebrew text is *ex hypothesi* of unknown meaning, or the sense which in the past has been ascribed to it is now taken to be a wrong one. Thus, to cite one of the first examples set out in the book just mentioned, a case of Hebrew *k-l-m*, *maklim*, traditionally taken to mean "to put to shame", may now, it has been suggested, be taken as "to speak", on the basis of the Arabic cognate *k-l-m* with this sense [1]). Sometimes new identifications of this kind imply not words of common proto-Semitic descent but loan-words, and in such cases they depend rather on the methods of Etymology C. This may be so, for instance, with the identification of *śᵉkiyot* at Isa. ii 16, traditionally "views" but now held to be "ships"; the identification appears to imply that the word was an Egyptian one (or otherwise international), adopted into Ugaritic and also into Hebrew [2]).

There is no question in our present discussion of the validity of this method; all I want to point out is that its mode of operation is different from that of other types of etymological study. In particular, the acknowledgement that Etymology E is a valid operation within its own particular scope by no means entails the consequence that other types of etymology are important within the sphere of synchronic semantics—a difference which seemed to me to be sufficiently obvious [3]). One difference in particular should be noted. Etymology E is by the nature of the case concerned almost entirely with *gross* semantic differences: a word, formerly taken to mean "put to shame", is now supposed to mean "speak", and one traditionally understood as "views" is now identified as having the sense "ships". This is true of most cases where the appeal to Ugaritic or Arabic or Akkadian has brought about a drastic change of acceptation as against an older understanding of a word, or has furnished a meaning for a word formerly taken to be unintelligible. But exegetical and theological questions, including all of those treated in my *Semantics*, belong not to gross semantics but to fine semantics; we are concerned with the exact theological range of (say) *πίστις*, but nobody will (on the basis of Gothic or Hittite) tell us that it does not mean "faith" but rather "horse" or "boat". The validity of Etymology E can thus rightly be instanced (as was done in my book) as one mode in which etymology can elucidate meaning; but it has very little in common with the questions of theological semantics there under discussion.

---

1) *Comparative Philology*, pp. 14f.

2) *Ibid.*, index, no. 322.

3) This difference is missed by both Hill and Friedrich in their discussions of my argument, as cited above, p. 2, n. 1.

Etymology F: simple comparison of institutions with cognate names

I am doubtful whether Etymology F is a real case; all I can say is that, in the discussions about the value of etymology for biblical study in which I have been involved, this procedure has often been cited. If we have the Hebrew word *nabi'* "prophet", and we can set alongside it a similar term *nabīum* in Mesopotamia, is it not proper that the nature of the one institution should be used to elucidate the other? The weakness of etymologizing, namely the fact that it tends to drag in long *past* meanings into the present semantics of a word, would here be avoided: for the texts are fairly close to one another in time, the cultures are comparable, and the names in both areas are likely to be derived in a similar sense. Such is the case put forward. It is, then, a matter of comparison of similar social situations or institutions, which also bear the same or cognate names. Is it not probable that the comparison of the two sets of phenomena would assist us in the understanding of both? The answer of course is "yes". It is a question, however, whether this is a real case of etymology; or, to put it another way, to include this would be to extend the term "etymology" far beyond the point where it continues to be distinctive and therefore useful. Comparisons like those between Hebrew prophets and comparable figures at Mari are justified whether or not we have the same word, or similar words, for similar institutions; for instance, the comparison of biblical covenants with the Hittite treaties is certainly justified in principle, although we have no common linguistic elements such as those applying to both Israel and Mari. Conversely, the fact that we find related words does not *in itself* prove much, or at least it does not prove that the phenomena named are the same; decisions about the degree of similarity of institutions are dependent on the comparison of the things themselves and are neither proved nor disproved by the community of the terms used. Thus, in spite of the agreed importance of the kind of study to which the title of Etymology F has been assigned, such study does nothing in itself to justify the validity or importance of etymology in the sense (or senses) generally attributed to the word. What is perhaps more correct is the observation that in the study of early historical periods work of the kind I have called Etymology F is often found in association with true etymology, e.g. type A.

Some Generalizations

We have thus separated out six different types of operation, any of which might be termed etymological. I am myself inclined to say that from the types here identified four are real cases, viz. A-D; E is not a different case, but an application, sometimes of C but more often of A; and F is not a real case at all, but rather something found in association with etymology. If one takes the discussions of words in typical Hebrew dictionaries, I think one would find that these various types of statement are found, often mixed up, and with a very considerable degree of variation from one word to another.

But surely we are entitled to generalize and say: there is no single clearly marked entity, which is etymology. Rather, the term etymology is a loose—and now also a traditional—designation for a somewhat ill-assorted bundle of different linguistic operations. If this is right, it will have justified our procedure in this paper, in not starting out from a "correct" definition of etymology, but proceeding rather from the ways in which people would generally use the word. I think that, if a clear and strict definition had to be given, it would have to be a definition not of etymology but of historical linguistics, or of the generative relations between roots and formed words, or things like that; then, within these relations thus defined, one could point to the matters which have traditionally been assigned to etymology. But etymology as such can now be seen to be no longer a strictly definable subject. This, incidentally, may well have a connection with the fact that modern treatises on general linguistics often say very little about it [1]). Again, any strict linguistic definition of etymology would probably not be conterminous with the general usage of the term.

Putting it in another way, the concepts with which etymology has generally been associated have been relativized by our analysis. It is no longer possible to say that such and such is "the" etymology of a word, or that the word "etymologically means" such and such a thing. At the very least one would have to specify which of the various kinds of etymological operation one had in mind; or else, perhaps, one could reach a definitive etymological description only if one made sure that all of them had been covered. Or, again, we have to avoid being misled by the etymology of the word *etymology* itself; we have inherited this

[1]) Cf. Malkiel, *Essays*, pp. 175ff.: Palmer, *op. cit.*, p. 300.

term from a pre-scientific period in the history of language study, from a time when it was supposed (with varying degrees of seriousness) that etymological studies would lead to the *etymon*, the true and "genuine" meaning. There is in fact no such thing as the *etymon* of a word, or there are as many kinds of *etymon* as there are kinds of etymological research.

If on the other hand we turn from the concept of the *etymon* to that of *origins*, this also has to be seen as greatly relativized. In fact none of the types of etymology which we have outlined give access to an ultimate origin. On the contrary, they tend to lead to an infinite regress, for there is no origin beyond which there is not a still earlier origin. In most types of etymology, *origin* can only mean that which is taken as the goal and scope for the purpose of this particular linguistic operation. Of the types in my analysis, the one which seems to have a most precise origin to deal with is Etymology C, for the adoption of a word from another language can be thought of as taking place at a precise time and with the sense obtaining at that time; though even then, as is obvious, the word has already a previous history in its own language. The type which appears to go farthest back towards the beginnings is Etymology A, but it would be hazardous to assert that the information it furnishes constitutes the true "origins". When we say "original" of a proto-Semitic form or meaning as disclosed under Etymology A, we really mean only "original in the sense of the farthest back we can go on the basis of the group of data taken as the base line for this case".

This in turn has effects on our conception of the proto-language, in our case proto-Semitic, to which Etymology A gives access : the proto-language, like historical states of language, is subject to relativity. The reconstructions are founded on the limited groups of facts from extant languages taken to provide the bases; the proto-language is the minimal necessary hypothesis which can explain or account for the known material in a group of cognate languages. Similarly, one cannot know that the "original" state reconstructed on the base of extant forms with a common *'-m-r* will be exactly contemporaneous with the "original" state reconstructed on the basis of another set of forms, e.g. (let us say) forms with a common *w-th-b* or a common *g-l-š*. This is an additional reason why proto-Semitic is a construct of the research process, a necessary and valid construct, but not something we can treat as an actual language, on the same level as historical Hebrew or Arabic of any period. This in turn is important for the study of meanings: etymological reconstructions can be carried out for this word or for that, but not simultaneously for the entire vocabulary; in this sense etymology is a word-isolating process.

But the meanings of words are functions of the choice of this word as against that within the stock of elements at one time. Etymology, at least in the conditions prevailing in the Semitic languages, is not likely to be able to reconstruct complete word-groups and semantic fields in the proto-Semitic stage, except perhaps for some very elementary instances, such as "nose-eyes-ears" and similar parts of the body, and so its conclusions about meanings must remain very hypothetical. Who, after all, could even imagine a proto-Semitic sentence containing the root *'-m-r* with the sort of meanings ascribed to it—quite justifiably, no doubt—in the citation earlier given from the Baumgartner dictionary? It is not surprising, then, that no one thinks of writing stories or doing prose composition in proto-Semitic, or in proto-Indo-European either.

Thus, if we try to restate in terms of modern language study that which was traditionally known as etymology, we might have to say something like this: Etymology is the traditional term for several kinds of study, working upon words as the basic units and interested in the explication of them in relation to similar elements which are historically earlier, which are taken within the scope of the study as "original", which appear to be more basic as units of meaning, or which appear to have a prior place in some generative process.

We thus have to revise somewhat the judgement cited earlier in this paper to the effect that etymology is a historical study; this, as we now see, is not necessarily true of all kinds of etymology. Moreover, even in those kinds of etymology which are truly historical processes, working with diachronic categories of before and after, much etymology has not been unbiassedly historical, but has essayed history with a bias, a bias in favour of that which is earliest and most original. As we would have to express it now, a truly historical survey of the development of words is perfectly possible and desirable, but it would be something different from that which has most generally been the interest, and also the attraction, of etymology.

When we consider the amount of interest and curiosity that has gone into etymology, we see that one of its main hidden attractions has lain not in historical origins but in the achievement of what may be called *transparency* [1]. "Transparency, very roughly, means that the user feels

---

[1]) For an analysis of one biblical Hebrew word-group in these terms see the writer's

not only that the word has a meaning but that you can see through it to some kind of reason why it has that meaning" [1]). To take a commonly-cited example, English *glove* is opaque but German *Handschuh* (containing elements for *hand* and *shoe*) is transparent. Thus, as I suggested, *pesel* "not only means 'graven image' (of a god) but can be seen to mean it because it suggests the verb *pasal* 'cut or carve stone' " [2]). Now, one reason for the great appeal of etymology is that it appears to furnish a transparency of this kind to words. This is another way in which the customary interest in "origins" has been only in part historical. Mere historical origins are of much less interest to people if they do not also increase the apparent transparency of words, if they do not appear in this way to "add to" the meaning already known : if etymology, working on the word *man*, shows only that this was derived from an original word *man*, the meaning of which also was "man", people are not very excited by this discovery. But if they discover that the opaque *hekal* can be provided with a transparency through the Sumerian meaning "great house", then they feel that they understand the word better (even if, as I have argued, the Sumerian sense is irrelevant for the acceptation in Hebrew); and the same is the case with *odontology*, *misanthrope*, *technocracy* and the rest.

Thus, behind the human interest in etymology (and this would seem to apply both to popular etymology and to scholarly etymology, in so far as the latter has an effect upon the popular consciousness) lies one of the fundamental facts about human language : the arbitrariness of the relationship between the sign and the thing signified, between the word and the thing that it designates. There is no reason in the nature of things why the entity dog is designated by the sign *dog* and not by the sign *cat*. Etymology, however, gives the appearance of reducing this arbitrariness of language : the dog is called *dog* because someone at an earlier stage called it *dog*—which, within its own limits, is a quite proper observation. When words are made derivationally transparent, this appears to reduce the arbitrariness, the conventionality, of language. If you know Greek ὀδούς and Greek λόγος, then you can see a reason why this science is called *odontology*, why it is this word rather than some other word. The rationality thus apparently imparted

---

"The Image of God in the Book of Genesis—a Study of Terminology", *Bulletin of the John Rylands Library* li (1968-9), pp. 11-26; also SAWYER, *ibid.*, p. 39.

1) BARR, "The Image of God", p. 17.

2) BARR, ibid.

to language by derivational transparency is, however, an illusion; it is only the moving back of the form-sense relationship to a slightly earlier stage, at which once again it is just as arbitrary: ὀδούς and λόγος are just as arbitrary, just as opaque, as *odontology* would have been if we had not known of its derivation, as English *tooth* and *word* are in our present speech.

Thus, to summarize, we can now easily see how one can at the same time accept the importance of etymological study and also point to the limitations of it for many other kinds of linguistic question. If one admits its importance for the identification of unusual words in Hebrew, this belongs to Etymology E; but this admission does not contradict the need to restrict the influence of etymological reasoning on exegesis in general, since this latter would commonly rest upon a different operation, such as type A. It is obvious, again, that in the understanding of Hebrew a great importance attaches to the ability to analyse the relations between the root morpheme and the vowel/prefix/affix pattern, but this belongs to yet another type of etymology (type D).

Again, much depends on what is the major purpose of our study. If our aim is primarily the reconstruction of the prehistoric stages of a language or a language group, then we may work mainly with etymology A. But if our primary interest lies in the understanding of meanings in biblical Hebrew, then the importance of etymology becomes considerably less. Etymology E, as we have seen, when properly used may through the evidence of other Semitic languages bring about a drastic change of acceptation as against the older understanding of words; but such work belongs to gross semantics, while most exegetical and theological questions belong to fine semantics. It is rather ironic that some of those who have defended the importance of etymology for semantic analysis have tried to do so by emphasizing the importance of the nuance in word meanings. In fact the nuance is the last thing that can be obtained from really etymological study; it is from the text, and not from etymology (of any type whatever) that knowledge about nuances is to be gained.

Naturally, the history of words and their meanings is of importance —if we know it; but this is by no means the same thing as etymology. Etymology, in any strict understanding of the term, may tell us only a little about this history of words. One of the values of Etymology A, as we saw, is that by reconstructing a probable prehistoric state it enables us to envisage the path which a word has travelled before it reached its earliest evidenced state (in our case, in biblical Hebrew);

this, though a service to the historical imagination, is only a small part of actual history. Only in Etymology B, where a word is followed through its history by evidence from extant documents, is historical information in the full sense furnished, and similarly in type C. But even in these the process cannot be truly historical if it is governed by a bias of curiosity and interest in favour of the beginnings of the process rather than the process as a whole. For word history, as it affects the exegesis of texts, it is commonly more important to know the more recent previous development than to know the earliest. In the New Testament, from which the examples in *Semantics* mostly come, it is more important to know a word's history in the Hellenistic age than to know its meaning in Homer, and much more important to know its meaning in Homer than to know its meaning in pre-Greek or in proto-Indo-European. And in some other respects, as has been indicated, etymology is not a particularly historical operation at all. Thus we may say that the relation of etymology to history is in parts ambiguous; and, though modern etymology involves a historical perspective, much of the resultant etymological analysis is not particularly historical in character.

Popular etymology

With these remarks we now finally come back to the matter of popular etymology. As has been mentioned, the etymological consciousness is not peculiar to the modern world. Even a casual acquaintance with Talmud and Midrash, especially the latter, reveals a very considerable cultivation of etymological interpretation. Long lists of etymological explanations of biblical names were furnished, handed down or compiled by scholars like Philo, Origen, Jerome and Isidore of Seville. In these scholars of the Greco-Roman world one sees the flowing together of the two major streams of ancient etymological interest, the Greco-Roman and the Jewish. The question therefore can legitimately be asked, as we have seen : is there not a danger that in limiting the significance of etymology for biblical interpretation we may be cutting ourselves off from something that to the men of the Bible themselves, and still more to their followers, was deeply significant? Or, in still wider terms, is not the etymological instinct one of the ways in which the phenomenon of language in fact works upon the human psyche?

Such questions are indeed reasonable, but we shall answer them in the same way as the previous set: basically, something different is here meant by the word *etymology*. We are now talking not of modern scholarly etymology, disciplined by historical and classificational criteria, but of something coming closer to popular etymology or belonging entirely to it. While something of the motivation, the interest and the curiosity is common to both types, the discipline and the science attach to one only. We can expand these considerations briefly as follows :

1. One of the factors, indeed doubtless the most important one, which favoured the interest in etymology during biblical times was the character of the Hebrew personal name, which unlike our English personal name was often an intelligible utterance, a phrase or a sentence. In this sense Hebrew names can be regarded as "transparent"; they seem to "mean something" [1]. The fact that this was true of the average name in historical Israel encouraged the provision of etymologies for names of the early saga. Paradoxically, however, the Bible is most active in providing etymological explanations of names just where the correct explanations lay beyond the reach of the writers, because the names were in fact foreign, or were received by tradition from earlier cultures, or belonged to types which in historical times were no longer productive—or indeed just because the purpose of the etymology was not so much to "explain" the name in itself as to link it with some legendary feature already present in the narrative tradition—as is the case with the familiar explanation of the name Moses, "I drew him out from the water". Conversely, as FICHTNER remarked some years ago [2], it is quite unusual for the Bible to provide etymological explanations of the customary names of the central biblical period.

2. Thus, though etymological explanations of names are very noticeable in the early traditions and especially in Genesis, it is important to avoid exaggerating this into an idea that the Hebrew consciousness in biblical times was a highly etymological one. On the contrary, apart from the explanation of some names, and apart from general exploitations of assonance and word-similarities, etymological explanation is used in the Hebrew Bible only within modest limits (and the same, interestingly enough, is true of the New Testament). Within the Old Testament the later texts which actualized earlier traditions, like the Deuteronomy in its use of older legal material,

---

[1]) Some of this ground is surveyed in my "The Symbolism of Names in the Old Testament", *Bulletin of the John Rylands Library* lii (1969-70), pp. 11-29.

[2]) In *Vetus Testamentum* vi (1956), pp. 372-96.

or the Chronicler in his use of material from Kings, seem to have developed only very sparingly, if at all, the etymological interpretation of the older stage. One reason for this is that etymological interpretation naturally goes along with a text conceived of as already fixed and inspired; in other words, it goes along with conceptions of literality and verbal inspiration—and also of allegory [1]). The limited character of the etymologizing explanation of words in the Bible is clearly seen by contrast with post-biblical times, when etymological interpretation rises to very much greater proportions: one can often find ten cases or so on a page of the Babylonian Talmud. Thus, to sum up this point, the fact that an etymological interest exists within the pages of the Hebrew Bible cannot be generalized or magnified into the idea that the writers cherished a strong etymological consciousness. The contrary is the case, and the biblical books are in general less etymologically interested than the later exegesis of them came to be, and especially so if one leaves on one side the explanation of names of persons and places, which forms almost the sole centre of interest for biblical etymology, words other than proper nouns receiving on the whole very little attention of this kind.

3. Moreover, there is yet another qualification which should be placed upon the etymological interest of the Bible. On the one hand, the material which might be classed as etymological merges almost imperceptibly with plays on assonances, word similarities and other associations. The double use of *š-k-ḥ* at Ps. cxxxvii 5 is a poetic exploitation of homonymy; the use of similar words in Isa. v 7 (*mišpaṭ—mišpaḥ, ṣ*ᵉ*daqa—ṣ*ᵉʿ*aqa*) is a poetic exploitation of assonances and word-similarities; the juxtapositions of *qayiṣ* and *qeṣ*, of *šaqed* and *šoqed*, in famous passages of Amos and Jeremiah, belong to a process of divination by word-suggestion. None of these are what we would, by any stretch of the sense of the term, designate as etymology; but they represent the mental milieu in which ancient biblical etymology existed, and no one at the time would have thought of drawing a distinction between etymology and this group of uses of language. Etymology was no more explicit, no more disciplined, no more clear in its scope and purpose, than were these various poetic and literary techniques. Biblical etymology, then, is no more than a special case of the literary use of linguistic associations.

That this is so may be confirmed by the observation that many of the

---

[1]) On this cf. my *Old and New in Interpretation* (1966), pp. 107f.

biblical etymologies of names are pretty obviously "wrong"—and I do not mean wrong by our modern criteria of historical linguistics, but wrong as analysis of words and roots by the criteria which were implicit in the language structure itself and which, we may with good reason suppose, must have been natural and indigenous at the time. To interpret the name Noah not on the basis of the root *nuaḥ* but on the basis of *n-ḥ-m*; to interpret Zebulon on the basis of the root *z-b-d* "donate", while at the same time unabashedly giving another explanation based on *z-b-l*; and to interpret Samuel on the basis of *š-'-l* "ask"—these and other such cases show that for the indigenous etymological sense word-similarity was enough: etymology was a play on word-similarity, rather than a serious analysis of root meanings. *z-b-d* was close enough to *z-b-l* for it not to matter, just as *miśpaḥ* was close enough to *mišpaṭ* for it not to matter whether they were (in our terms) "the same root" or just words that displayed an interesting similarity and assonance. When post-biblical etymologists and interpreters confused one laryngal with another, or gave an explanation that depended on one consonant when the word in the text had another—e.g. in an example such as:

> B. Ber. 57a: הרואה הספד בחלום מן השמים חסו עליו ופדאוהו
> *ha-ro'e hesped baḥalom min ha-šamayim ḥasu 'alaw u-pᵉda'uhu*
> "If one perceives a funeral oration in a dream, mercy will be vouchsafed to him from heaven and he will be redeemed"

—they were in fact following in the lines which the biblical writers themselves had followed. It is mistaken to evaluate such practices as direct evidence in historical phonetics, e.g. as evidence that at the time of writing the laryngals were not distinguished; for the purpose of the interpretation it is sufficient that the laryngals (or, respectively, other groups of sounds) were perceived as similar enough to establish some relation.

To sum up this point, the etymology (so-called) of the men of the Bible is more a kind of poetry, a kind of conceit, even a kind of humour, than something comparable with what we today call linguistic study. The appreciation of it may, accordingly, belong rather to literary criticism than to philology or linguistics [1]).

---

[1]) On this see K. K. Ruthven, "The Poet as Etymologist", *Critical Quarterly* xi (1969), pp. 9-37, including criticism of the present writer on pp. 34 f.

4. It is therefore entirely proper that we should take an interest in the etymological interests of the men of the Bible, and of the post-biblical exegesis, both Jewish and Christian, of their writings. But this can be no more than a historical question. We may rightly ask ourselves, what were the etymological associations which they in their time might have seen in this word or that?—and for this question the evidence will have to be found in the world of ancient etymology [1]). But it would be entirely unhistorical and anachronistic to suppose that any amount of ancient etymology would serve as justification for the application to biblical words of etymological information which *we*, working from our completely different historical-linguistic perspective, might detect [2]).

And thus the fact of etymology within the Bible does not in itself justify a concern with modern etymology as a proper semantic concern of the modern scholar. The latter is a quite different matter, and one that requires to have its own separate justification. There is indeed every reason to recognize that the instinct for popular etymology is an element in the basic psychological functioning of any language. Occasionally it has been suggested to me that the etymological interpretation of biblical language by modern scholars which I examined in my *Semantics* might be justified as a sort of modern midrash, a natural consequence of the fact that scraps of historical linguistic information and etymological consciousness are now innate in the psyche of modern man. Whether this is so or not, these interpretations never represented themselves in this way and would never have been accepted if they had so done. Even if etymologizing fancy is inherent in the human soul, this does not form a basis for just *any* use of modern

---

[1]) Suggestions might also be found in such work as J. Vendryes, "Pour une étymologie statique", *Bulletin de la Société de linguistique de Paris* xlix (1953), pp. 1-19. As the title suggests, this article, recognizing that the past accepted framework of etymology has been a diachronic one, suggests a synchronic approach, in which etymology would take into account the relations between words in one contemporaneous state of the language. The implications of these suggestions have not been taken up in the present version of this paper.

[2]) In fact few or none of the arguments which I in *Semantics* criticized for "etymologizing" based themselves on the facts of the *ancient* etymological tradition, nor did they show much awareness of the importance of that tradition. They certainly did not attempt to show that the alleged etymological relations had been historically perceived. Thus the argument we are now considering, i.e. the idea that the fact of ancient etymology might justify the practice of modern etymologizing, is an entirely *a posteriori* justification of the latter, and not one that was much in evidence at the time.

etymological information, nor does it justify the placing of such information within a genre reminiscent of ancient midrash. One might by analogy say that a natural function of the human psyche in its awareness of the past is the instinct to manufacture exaggerations, legends and myths; but the fact that the process may be natural does not raise exaggerations, legends and myths to the level of history. Similarly the fact that etymology may be a natural function does not constitute any guarantee of its right application. And if popular etymology belongs to the sphere of poetry and of fancy, the fact of this can be properly acknowledged; but along with this it must be recognized that within these spheres one cannot use the concept of "validity" as argument or proof that has usually been sought in the theological use of the Bible [1]).

With this we must end the hasty review of our problem. Among the various issues which have been mentioned, the one which lies deepest, and which forms the storm-centre of the disagreements about etymology within biblical study in our time, is the question of the arbitrary character of language. The fascination for etymology, as has been suggested, is the attraction of a means by which the arbitrariness of language appears to be reduced or removed; the effect of this is to make language appear to reflect the reality of things as they are, and to ally the language of the Bible with conceptions of authority, with a basically authority-seeking approach to reality. Though modern etymology in the scientific sense represents a variety of different processes, and though it is in itself, within these different modes and within proper limits, an entirely valid and positive process, the possibility that it may overcome, or even alleviate, the arbitrariness of language in its relation to reality is a hope that should now be abandoned.

---

[1]) These remarks among other things answer some of the arguments of K. K. RUTHVEN, ibid., pp. 34f. He in general misunderstands my position, not least in that he takes seriously things like the connection between *beśora* "good news" and *baśar* "flesh" (*Semantics*, p. 159 n.), which were intended as a *reductio ad absurdum* and would, I think, be so taken by all informed readers. They are examples, invented by me, of the joke function of etymologies—on this, incidentally, with reference to Talmudic passages like the one cited above, I am indebted for suggestions to my friend Mr Raphael LOEWE. As Mr RUTHVEN says, "connections that are felt to exist" are important facts, and I never doubted this; what I denied in *Semantics* was that the connections, cited and used by theological interpreters, had ever been "felt to exist" in any authentic and relevant current of usage of the languages concerned.

ISAIAH LIV: THE MULTIPLE IDENTITY OF THE PERSON ADDRESSED

BY

W. A. M. BEUKEN

Amsterdam

The question who is the woman addressed throughout Isa. liv, offers the opportunity of performing a style-critical exegesis of this chapter, an approach which appears to be more and more fruitful with regard to the prophecies of Deutero-Isaiah (DI). Moreover, it may demonstrate the importance of the biblical phenomenon of the corporate personality, a concept to which the late H. W. ROBINSON has most meritoriously drawn the attention [1]). So it seemed suitable to deal with this subject at this joint meeting of the British and Dutch Societies for the Study of the Old Testament.

Our question is legitimate because the facts are striking. Throughout the chapter the form of address is constantly the feminine singular, but the name of the woman is not mentioned anywhere. The only names which occur are Israel (5) and Noah (9). Neither in the preceding chapter nor in the next one is this same woman to be found. DUHM has welcomed this lack of an explicit mention as a support for his thesis that the Servant Songs have been inserted later on into the framework of Ch. xl-lv. In his opinion, Ch. lii, where Zion-Jerusalem is brought the good tidings of God's return, continues in Ch. liv without the need of mentioning the name of the Holy City again [2]). From the present point of view, however, it is rather bold to suppose that the Servant Songs have been intercalated into their present context in such a way that they have no relation to the surrounding chapters and simply disrupt the train of thought [3]). Besides, the identity of the Servant himself is complicated enough to prevent us from easily passing over the question

---

[1]) H. W. ROBINSON, "The Hebrew Conception of Corporate Personality", in: *Werden und Wesen des Alten Testaments* (BZAW 66), Berlin 1936, pp. 49-62.

[2]) B. DUHM, *Das Buch Jesaja*, Göttingen 1968[5], p. 407.

[3]) Cf. the present author's: "Mišpāṭ. The First Servant Song and its Context", *VT* 22 (1972), pp. 1-30.

of the woman of Ch. lv. Finally, we see in Ch. xl 1-11 that the prophet leaves both the persons addressed and those speaking intentionally vague. The meaning of this obscurity is not our concern here, but important enough [1] to have us suspect that the lack of a name for the woman of Ch. liv is not devoid of sense.

By inquiring into her identity we do not deny that somehow she must be Zion as most modern translations [2], commentaries [3] and monographs [4] indicate in their superscription or explanation. The likeness with Zion is given by the context of the chapter, explicated by Paul in Gal. iv 27, where he cites vs. 1 and applies it to the Jerusalem above, and also by the Targum of Jonathan, where the name of Jerusalem has been woven into the text not less than five times [5]. Moreover, the chapter elaborates themes from the previous chapters xlix-lii, which regard Zion.—The question at issue, however, is this: do we give the richness of the chapter its due by identifying the person addressed exclusively as Jerusalem from the very outset? We should take stock of all the traits which combine to give us a picture of the woman who is the focus of the chapter. By so doing, we shall discover that the New English Bible (NEB), this widely discussed new translation, is at least not wrong in heading this chapter with the line 'Israel a light to the nations' [6].

So, this study will involve three parts. (I) We have to investigate whether the chapter may be considered as a literary unity, and to determine its structure. (II) By pursuing the thematic connections we shall come to see the variety of shapes and forms under which the

---

[1] Cf. on this subject: CL. WESTERMANN, *Das Buch Jesaja. Kap. 40-66* (ATD), Göttingen 1966.

[2] *Nieuwe Vertaling van het Nederlandsch Bijbelgenootschap* (NBG), *Bible de Jérusalem* (BJ), *Pattloch Bibel* (PB), *New American Bible* (NAB). The RSV refers to Gal. iv 27.

[3] FRANZ DELITZSCH, *Commentar über das Buch Jesaja* (BC), Leipzig 1889⁴; C. R. NORTH, *The Second Isaiah*, Oxford 1964; J. L. MCKENZIE, *Second Isaiah* (AB), Garden City 1968.

[4] J. VAN DER MERWE, *Pentateuchtradisies in die prediking van Deuterojesaja*, Groningen 1956, p. 115; Y. KAUFMANN, *The Babylonian Captivity and Deutero-Isaiah*, New York 1970, p. 186; C. STUHLMUELLER, *Creative Redemption in Deutero-Isaiah* (An. Bibl. 43), Rome 1970, p. 118.

[5] In vss. 1 (twice). 10.15.17.

[6] Cf. L. G. RIGNELL, who, from his interpretation of the Servant as being Israel, sees a strong connection between Ch. liii and Ch. liv since the former deals with Israel's humiliation, the latter with her glory: *A Study of Isaiah Ch. 40-55* (Lunds Universitets Årsskrift, N.F. Avd. 1, Bd. 52, Nr. 5), Lund 1956, pp. 84 f.

woman appears on the scene. (III) Once we shall have established her multiple identity, we may ask ourselves how the idea of corporate personality has been realized in this particular pericope.

I. Unity and structure of the chapter

The intrinsic unity of the chapter was for the older commentators a matter of sure evidence [1]. However, since the opinion that the book was written according to a definite plan no longer found general acceptance, scholars have been strongly divided in their marking off the various sections. Especially the so-called flysheets-theory opened the way to parceling out the sixteen chapters into a great number of unities [2]. With regard to Ch. liv we find authors who divide the chapter into four pericopes [3]. However, a twofold division is most widely accepted (1-10.11-17), proposed e.g. by North, but even today there is no general agreement : McKenzie considers the chapter as a unity in which only vss. 15-17 form an expansion [4], while Westermann separates the second part into two independent sections [5]. As to my own opinion, I would argue for the unity of the chapter. I have come to this position, first because Ch. liv is clearly marked off from Ch. liii and from Ch. lv by the difference of the person addressed. Only in Ch. liv and throughout the chapter a single woman is addressed. In the preceding fourth Servant Song she does not occur, while the second half of the last verse of Ch. liv prepares the way for the change-over to the plural form of address, which is found throughout Ch. lv [6]. As long as there are no strong indications for one or more literary hinges within the chapter, the unity of the pericope ought to be our point of departure. Differences of literary genre are not, of themselves, indications of

---

1) E.g. Delitzsch, o.c.

2) A survey of the history of this question is offered by North, *o.c.*, pp. 4-12.

3) Vss. 1-6. 7-10. 11-14a. 14b-17 : Duhm, *o.c.*; L. Köhler, *Deuterojesaja stilkritisch untersucht* (BZAW 37), Giessen 1923.

4) O.c., p. 140 .

5) O.c., p. 223 : vss. 11-13a. 13b-17.

6) Cf. K. Elliger, *Deuterojesaja in seinem Verhältnis zu Tritojesaja* (BWANT 63), Stuttgart 1933, pp. 137-140. He connects to it the conclusion that the chapter stems from Trito-Isaiah, on grounds of topics, style and use of words (pp. 143-148, 152-163, 266 f.). We need not go into this matter as we intend to study the intrinsic unity of the chapter. Now and again we may adduce arguments from Ch. xl-lv as a whole. We are justified to do so since these chapters unmistakably constitute the present context of Ch. liv.

independent pericopes. They may play their role within the formal and thematic unity of the whole composition, a role of differentiating the pericope, not one of dividing it. It is generally accepted that the prophecies of DI constitute larger compounds, in which he uses a great variety of literary genres, independently adapting them to the train of his thought. So, I consider it the task of the exegete to elaborate and to make meaningful the unity of the chapter as it presents itself at first glance, unless further research obliges him to reverse his initial impression.

If the unity of Ch. liv is basically given by the continuity of the one person addressed, the structural articulation is determined in the first instance by the difference of the persons speaking. Therefore, the main division lies before vs. 7 : in vss. 1-6 the prophet is speaking, in vss. 7-17 it is God himself.

In spite of the messenger formulae which conclude vss. 1 and 6, the first passage (1-6) as a whole must be seen as spoken by the prophet. Nowhere does God appear speaking in the first person. Moreover, in vss. 5. 6a someone evidently makes statements about God. The messenger formulae put into God's mouth exclusively the lines which are immediately preceding, i.e. the reasons for joy and fearlessness found in vs.1bβ ("For the children of the desolate one will be more than the children of her that is married" [1]) and in vs.6b ("Verily, the wife of one's youth, will she be rejected ?" [2]). This is achieved not by a change of speaker, from the first person of the prophet to the first person of God, as is usual, but by a change of the person addressed to the person spoken about : in vss.1abα and 6a Israel is directly addressed, in the next lines, concluded by the messenger formulae, she is referred to. This particular use of the formula citandi leads to the effect that God, as it seems, is not present on the stage. The prophet himself apparently addresses the woman, summons her to joy without fear and refers to the Lord as the source of his gladdening message by twice formulating exclusively the reasons for his call in words directly spoken by God. Köhler already came to the finding that DI is considerably free in using the various formulae citandi either in introductory or

---

[1]) Scripture is generally quoted according to RSV except where we were at variance.

[2]) This interpretation of *kî* was first proposed by Duhm, o.c., p. 409 : "*we-kî* ist wie *'ap-kî* Gen. iii 1 ein Ausruf ungläubigen Staunens 'und dass !' ". Subsequently, it has been accepted by many others, e.g. : E. König, *Historisch-kritisches Lehrgebäude der hebräischen Sprache*, II 2, Leipzig 1897, § 353b; North, o.c., p. 250.

parenthetic or concluding positions [1]). His twofold use of the messenger formula here is a most striking example. Nowhere else in his prophecies are sentences marked by the messenger formula found in which these three phenomena occur together: (1) absence of God speaking in the first person, (2) Israel is not addressed in the second person but referred to in the third, (3) the immediate context speaks about God in the third person. All three of these facts combined lead to the effect that the messenger formula no longer characterizes the whole prophecy as God's direct message. Only the motivations contain God's words and the prophet refers to them as to the very roots of his summons to jubilation.

The second part of the chapter, vss. 7-17, is characterized by God's speaking in the first person to Israel in the second person. The first person referring to God is absent only in vss. 13f., the second person feminine for Israel occurs in all verses [2]). Twice the messenger formula is used (8.10) and at the end (17) the concluding term *n^{e}'um yhwh* [3]) marks the pericope off from the next chapter, which opens with a new address in the plural.

The place of the messenger formulae, however, leads to a second remark. They occur only in the first section of the second part, concluding the announcement of salvation (7f.) and the following comparison (9f.), which elaborates the everlasting character of God's new *ḥesed*. Moreover, in vs. 11 the woman is addressed again with a set of three qualifications ("O afflicted one, tempest-driven and not comforted"), comparable to that of vs. 1. Finally, from vs. 11 on new themes are broached. Whereas the first section elaborates the motif of the forsaken woman of the first part, the second section is less clearly connected to the speech of the prophet. All these data together have led many scholars to assume an original break between vss. 10 and 11. In my view, however, there is no need for such an assumption. The messenger formulae characterize the first section as words of God transmitted by the prophet. The new emphatic call upon the woman in vs. 11 combined with the lack of any messenger

1) O.c., pp. 102-109.

2) God mentions his own name twice but this need not surprise us since it is a common phenomenon with all the prophets. In vs. 13 *yhwh* may stand metri causa, in vs. 17 for the sake of variation within the parallelism.

3) This is the only text in DI where the term has a concluding function. In all other instances (xli 14; xliii 10.12; xlix 18; lii 5 twice; lv 8) it is parenthetic and carries on the course of God's speaking.

formula in vss. 11-17 marks the second section as a personal speech of God. Thus, the chapter as a whole offers a climatic progress of the persons who announce to the woman the new times of her salvation. In the first half (1-6) the prophet speaks: the only lines spoken by God are two motivations for fearless joy, in themselves oracles of salvation, which seem to come from an invisible God since he does not directly speak to the woman, but about her apparently to the prophet. In the first section of the second half (7-10) God addresses the woman directly, although by the mouth of the prophet, whose presence is still made felt by means of the messenger formulae. In the last section (11-17) God has entered the scene: filled with sorrow for her distress he calls upon the woman and announces to her unprecedented beauty and security. The climax of God's increasing presence to the woman is expressed by the twofold *hinnēh 'ānōkî* (11.16). BEGRICH has demonstrated that in the oracle of salvation *hinnēh* marks the promise of God's intervention and the certitude of his saving act [1]). Subsequent studies have pointed out that the terms *hinnēh 'ānōkî* or *hinnēnî* with the participle do not announce God's intervention as something in the future near or distant, but point to him as being present and active now in the life of those addressed [2]). So, in vs. 11 the lament of the woman, to which the threefold address may refer, is met first by God's laying the stones of the new city and secondly by his reminding her that his presence with her is that of the Creator.

If we go back for a moment to the first passage, the prophetic speech, we may pose the question whether here too a more detailed structure can be discerned on formal grounds. The messenger formulae simply lift out, as we have seen, the motivations of vss.1b and 6b. There are three series of imperatives and/or jussives with a negative (1a.2.4a), all of them followed by motivations (1b.3.5-6a) [3]). This threefold formal articulation, however, is not accompanied by a thematic division because there are only two themes: the woman as mother (1-3) and as wife (4-6). Now, the first motivation anticipates the theme

---

1) J. BEGRICH, *Studien zu Deuterojesaja* (Th. Büch. 20), München 1963², pp. 15-18.

2) A. PETITJEAN, "La Mission de Zorobabel et la Reconstruction du Temple. Zach. III, 8-10", *EThL* 42 (1966), pp. 40-71, esp. 41 f.

3) The *kî*-sentences of vs. 4 seem to be a kind of elaboration of the call 'fear not' and 'be not confounded'. At the same time, they prepare the motivation of vs. 5 since *'ălûmayik* provides the basis for *bō'ălayik*, *'almᵉnûtayik* for *gō'ălēk*.

of the forsaken wife by the word *b^e'ûlâ* (1b.cf.5). Therefore, vs.1 may be seen as a kind of superscription to the whole passage. While opening the mother-section it simultaneously announces the theme of the abandoned wife. In this way, the threefold series of imperatives and motivations appropriately goes together with the two themes that dominate the passage. The change from mother to wife is the prevailing structural datum since the latter offers the link to the second part of the chapter, the speech of God himself.

II. Thematic connections

1. *The appeal of the prophet* (*1-6*)

The two sections which depict the woman as mother and wife are perfectly balanced by a set of three characteristics for each function given her by the prophet:

mother	*'ăqārâ*	(1)	wife	*'ălûmayik*	(4)
	lō' yālādâ	(1)		*'alm^enûtayik*	(4)
	lō'-ḥālâ	(1)		*'iššâ 'ăzûbâ*	(6)

Moreover, both paragraphs contain a word by which God himself characterizes the woman:

šômēmâ (1) and *'ēšet n^e'ûrîm* (6).

The three epithets of the mother are synonymous while the three of the wife are not: she cannot at the same time be unmarried [1]),

[1]) With regard to *'ălûmayik*, A. Schoors ("Two Notes on Isaiah xl-lv", *VT* 21 (1971), pp. 503-505) has raised the question: how is 'the shame of youth' to be understood? Assuming a Hebrew root *'lm* that is cognate to Ugaritic *ġlm* = servant he proposes the translation 'the shame of your bondage'. —In our eyes, however, the context, as will be shown, points to the traditional meaning 'youth' in the sense of being nubile. So, the shame would consist in this: while being an adult girl she is living without husband. Cf. F. Brown, S. R. Driver and Ch. A. Briggs, *A Hebrew and English Lexicon of the Old Testament* (BDB), Oxford 1906, s.v. *'lm* II : "perh. orig. *be mature* (sexually)"; W. Gesenius and F. Buhl, *Handwörterbuch über das Alte Testament* (GB), Berlin 1915[17], s.v. *'almâ* : "bezeichnet lediglich das Mädchen als mannbares". Similarly L. Köhler and W. Baumgartner, *Lexicon in Veteris Testamenti Libros* (KB), Leiden 1953. Consequently, M. Buber translates 'die Schande deiner Ledigkeit' : *Bücher der Kündung* verdeutscht von M. Buber gemeinsam mit F. Rosenzweig, Köln 1966[2], p. 170. The

widow and deserted. Obviously, these images are applicable to the woman only according to their common feature : she has to live without husband though her age requires such one (*'ălûmayik*) and though she has been married (*'almᵉnûtayik, 'iššâ 'ăzûbâ*). This set of images is more conspicuous than the first one because of their mutual discrepancy, which provokes attention and invites us to inquire after their proper meaning, i.e. their common element. Moreover, like their metaphorical content, so their theological content is considerably more substantial. They bring in their train three statements about God : (1) the young woman will not remain without husband; there is a *ba'al* for her, namely her Maker (5a), (2) likewise, there is a *gō'ēl* for the widow, the Holy One of Israel (5b), (3) the forsaken woman will be called back (6) [1]; it is Yhwh who will do so.

---

image should not be interpreted as referring to Israel's situation before she was married to Yhwh, i.e. to the sojourn in Egypt. "Jungfrauschaft besagt hier nicht Jungfräulichkeit im gewöhnlichen Sinne, sondern lediglich die durch Fernsein ihres Gemahls bewirkte Enthaltsamkeit im babylonischen Exil": J. FISCHER, *Das Buch Isaias II* (H. Schrift des A.T.), Bonn 1939, pp. 141 f. As the image of widowhood fails in that God did not die, so the image of nubility fails in that Israel had been married. Both images serve as far as they describe Israel as living without husband.

[1]) The problem of how to interpret *qᵉrā'āk* has been formulated by NORTH, o.c., p. 250 as follows : "Does this mean that Yahweh is now *recalling* Israel (the usual interpretation, so EVV) after the temporary separation of the exile ? Or does it mean that he *called* her to be his bride (the assumption in Jer. ii; Hos. ii) long ago... ? This second interpretation seems more probable and is supported by the form *qᵉrā'āḵ* ('he called you' pf.) and by the undoubted sense of the following context".—Nonetheless, we think that a presentic understanding (proposed by R. KITTEL in his revised edition of A. DILLMANN's *Der Prophet Jesaja* [KeHAT], Leipzig 1898⁶, h.l.) imposes itself. The first reason lies in the literary genre of the passage. WESTERMANN, in his thorough research of the salvation speeches in DI, has ascertained that the so-called *Begründung* of the oracle of salvation consists of two elements :" Das erste Glied bringt die Zuwendung Gottes zum Ausdruck, das zweite erst sein Eingreifen. Diese Zweiteilung hat ihre Entsprechung in der zweigliederigen Bitte im Klagepsalm.—Das Eingreifen Gottes im zweiten Teil ist fast durchweg in perfektischen Verben ausgesagt; sie bringen zum Ausdruck, dass das Eingreifen Gottes für den Flehenden im Augenblick des Zuspruches schon etwas Feststehendes, Abgeschlossenes ist. Diese perfektischen Verben zusammen mit dem Ruf 'Fürchte dich nicht!' sind das für den Heilszuspruch Charakteristische. Er ist *keine* Ankündigung, sondern eine Zusage, die im Augenblick dieses Zuspruches den Wandel schafft, gerade so wie das beim Ergehen des Heilszuspruches an Hanna in 1 Sam. 1 geschildert wird"; in : "Sprache und Struktur der Prophetie Deuterojesajas", in; *Forschung am Alten Testament. Gesammelte Studien* (Th. Büch. 24), München 1964, p. 119. (This paragraph of the article recapitulates his study: "Das Heilswort bei Deuterojesaja", *EvTh* 24 (1964), pp. 355-373). It is evident that vss. 5.6a correspond to the *Begründung*, vs.5 being the nominal senten-

A kind of incongruence similar to that we noticed for the epithets of the woman applies to those of God. He cannot at the same time be her first husband (*bō'ălayik*), kinsman (*gō'ălēk*) and the man who takes back his wife (*qerā'āk*). Moreover, the very concept of *gō'ēl* suggests that previously she had another husband who died and is to be succeeded by his kinsman. The image applies here in such a way that the notion of consanguinity is transformed into that of identity.

Cognizance should be taken of the fact that the series of epithets for the mother (1) goes without a similar set of corresponding characteristics for Yhwh which indicate how he will meet her present distress of being bereft of children.

With regard to the two epithets given by God himself to the woman, i.e. *šômēmâ* and *'ēšet ne'ûrîm*, we can also establish a climactic relation. While the first word describes her present miserable bereavement, the second one refers to her priveleges of old : she was the first choice of God, she was the wife of his youth [1]). In that original election lies the point of departure for a new relation of everlasting fidelity.

The foregoing style-critical observations have charted our course to an inquiry of the passage which will be more concerned with the content.—As for the first section, the woman is portrayed in traits that call to mind the mother of Israel, Sarah. VAN DER MERWE, in his thorough and careful inquiry into the Pentateuchal reminiscences in DI, allows the possibility that these verses are dependent on the patriarchal traditions of Genesis. The material leading to this conclusion consists of the following items :

1. The matriarchal barrenness seems to be alluded to in vs.1a, the wording of which recalls Gen. xi 30 : *wattehî šārāy 'ăqārâ 'ên lāh wālād* [2]).

---

ce, vs.6a the verbal one, while vs. 6b contains the result (*Folge* : ipf. !). The second reason lies in the context. What is at stake is that God calls his forsaken woman back now, not that he called her once. *qerā'āk* in parallelism to *kî timmā'ēs* paves the way for the second half of the chapter, where God actually returns to his wife.

[1]) Fidelity to the 'wife of one's youth' is both a wisdom recommendation (Prov. v 18) and a prophetic demand (Mal. ii 14 f.). Several times the prophets speak of Israel's youth (Hos. ii 17; Jer. ii 2; iii 4; xxxi 19; Ez. xvi 22.43.60) as being the period of her first engagement to Yhwh. Isa. liv 6 is the only place where *ne'ûrîm*, in the application of the metaphorical language, means God's youth. The passive *timmā'ēs* holds the application off and precludes the wonder that would arise from such statement.

[2]) O.c., p. 115 f. In his conclusion (p. 139) he modifies more in favour of this dependence.

2. The pledge of the land made to the patriarchs is alluded to by several terms in vs.3 :
-*yāmîn ûśᵉmô'l tiprōṣî* reminds of Gen. xxviii 14 : *ûpāraṣtā yāmmāh wāqēdmâ wᵉṣāpōnâ wānegbâ.*
-Vs.3b ("Your seed will expel nations and they will people desolate cities") combines, by the use of the verb *yrš*, the promise to the patriarchs and the longed for recovery of the land [1]).
Since VAN DER MERWE is quite detached in admitting relations between DI and the Pentateuch, we consider that his claim of the possibility of a like dependence of our verses stands on solid ground. We certainly have to apply the general results of his study to the particular dependence which engages our attention here. As he sees it, DI did not quote literally from the Pentateuch and "this independence in the use of words and thoughts must be explained by the fact that he adapted the tradition to the message he wanted to bring" [2]). If we take into account that this prophet was thoroughly familiar with the Pentateuch traditions and, at the same time, maintained an absolute freedom with regard to their content and wording, we must not underestimate the possible dependence which we found for our passage. Two external considerations allow us to see this dependence as a very probable one and to recognize Sarah in the mother figure as depicted here :
1. The affinity of this passage with Isa. li 1-3, where the prophet points out to Israel the barren Sarah by the side of the childless Abraham, who both have become the ancestors of a nation thanks to God's wonderful intervention. We should not omit noting that this history is taken up in order to proclaim to Zion the consolation of her imminent recovery [3]), as is the case with Ch. liv. The argument is all the weightier because this is the only text outside the Pentateuch in which Sarah is mentioned. Her entering on the scene certainly has to do with the growing influence of the Abraham tradition during the exile, as is reflected in the prophecies of Ezechiel and DI [4]), and in the coming into use of the expression "seed of Abraham" at the time of our prophet [5]).

---

1) O.c., p. 240.

2) O.c., p. 267.

3) A full inquiry of this passage can be found with VAN DER MERWE, o.c., pp. 103-124. Cf. also : N. A. VAN UCHELEN, "Abraham als Felsen (Jes. 51,1)", *ZAW* 80 (1968), pp. 183-191.

4) R. E. CLEMENTS, "Abraham", *ThWAT* I, pp. 59-62.

5) VAN DER MERWE, o.c., pp. 90-145.

2. The function of vss.1-3 in the first part of Ch. liv strenghtens the surmise that Israel is delineated here according to the traits which are characteristic of her ancestresses, more particularly as Sarah. The first section can only be understood fully by taking into account that it constitutes the counterpart of vss.4-6, which describe Israel as the wife of Yhwh. The very explicit portrayal of the latter makes up for the lack of determinate clearness which inheres in the portrayal of Israel as mother and explains it. In these six verses the prophet addresses himself to Israel as she has gone her way through history, from the dim outset of the barren mother to the wife who, while abandoned, is still aware of her old election. The sequence mother-wife may be illogical but is inspired by Israel's history and traditions, by the images that have come to typify the two earliest phases of her existence, the time of the wandering patriarchs and that of the life in the land.

Now that we have submitted the basic plan of our exegesis of vss. 1-3, we may add a few observations to those given by VAN DER MERWE and mentioned above. They will strengthen, as we hope, our explanation.

1. *yrš* occurs several times in the promises to the patriarchs of Genesis (Gen. xv 7f.; xxviii 4), but it is only in Gen. xxii 17; xxiv 60 that *zeraʿ* forms the subject. In the latter texts the promise of a multitudinous offspring precedes (Gen. xxii 17 : *harbâ 'arbeh*; cf. Isa. liv 1 : *rabbîm*), while the object is not 'the land', as in the former texts, but 'the gates of their enemies' and 'the gate of those who hate them'. The object of *yrš* in Isa. liv 3 is *gôyim*, which is the regular object of the same pledge as found in Deuteronomy and applied to Israel when she is about to enter the promised land (Num. xxxiii 52; Deut. iv 38; ix 1; xi 23; xii 2. 29; xviii 14; xix 1; xxxi 3). So, the portrayal of Israel-mother is transparent to her second shape, the woman who represents the people that had once dispossessed nations, had been dispossessed on its turn and now hopes to dwell again in the desolate cities.

2. *šômēmâ*, in contrasting parallelism to *beʿûlâ*, must be understood as 'desolate', which includes the two meaning-aspects of the root *šmm* : 'to be deserted by men' and 'to be appalled', viz. in face of the loneliness one has to endure [1]). Elsewhere [2]) I have tried to demonstrate that this

---

1) Cf. KB, p. 988. His lexicographical treatment of the root updates the statement of BDB, p. 1030 : "connection of meanings not clear" by suggesting that they are related as cause and consequence.

2) *Haggai—Sacharja 1-8. Studien zur Überlieferungsgeschichte der frühnachexilischen Prophetie* (Stud. Sem. Neerl. 10), Assen 1967, pp. 133 f.

verb is a characteristic term for a national lament ("The land is desolate"), which is alluded to in several oracles of Jeremiah and, more frequently, of Ezechiel [1]). The lament itself is found in Lam. i 13 : "He has left me desolate, faint all the day long". Here Jerusalem is the woman who wails.—DI's summons to rejoice may likewise be understood as an answer to a lament. So, from contemporary exilic terminology *šômēmâ* evokes the figure of both the land and the city lamenting their desolation. This conclusion is confirmed if we take a glance at DI's use the root *šmm*. In vs. 3, as in xlix 8.19, the immediate context refers to the desolate land, bare of inhabitants. Only in lii 14 the other meaning, to be appalled, prevails [2]).

3. A third confirmation comes from an inquiry of the motivation for rejoicing given by God : "For the children of the desolate one will be more than the children of her that is married" (1). As for its form, this sentence seems to be similar to that of several comparison maxims which are found in Proverbs and Qoheleth, e.g. :

> He who rebukes a man will afterward find more favor
> than he who flatters with his tongue (Prov. xxviii 23; cf. xvii 10; xviii 19; xxvi 16; xxvii 3)
> A little folly outweighs wisdom and honor (Qoh. x 1; cf. iv 17; vii 19).

All these similes have in common with Isa. liv that two things are compared from some point of view by means of the preposition *min*.

As for its content, the sentence of DI elaborates the theme of the sterile woman who, contrary to all expectations, becomes a mother. We may compare the following texts :

> Behold, you are barren and have no children;
> but you shall conceive and bear a son (Jud. xiii 3).
> He gives the barren woman a home,
> making her the joyous mother of children (Ps. cxiii 9).
> The barren one has borne seven,
> but she who has many children is forlorn (1 Sam. ii 5).

---

[1]) Jer. xii 11; xxxii 43. (cf. 36); Ez. vi 14; xii 20; xiv 15 f; xv 8; xxv 3; xxx 12; xxxiii 28 f.; xxxv 12; xxxvi 33-36; Zech. vii 14.

[2]) In Isa. xlii 14 the root *nšm* must be assumed, as most commentators do; cf. KB, p. 639.

The first text applies to one single woman, the wife of Manoah, and describes the wonderful change of situation that is about to enter her life because of God's intervention. The second text mentions the same event as a miracle that Yhwh is accustomed to work in favour of the poor of whom he takes care (cf. vss.6f. of the same psalm). In the last text (1 Sam.ii), the contrast between barrenness and fertility lies not only in the life of one woman (Hannah) or several women, but has also become an opposition between two classes of persons, as is clear from the context: "Yhwh makes poor and makes rich" (7). Apparently the tradition of God's intervention in the life of barren women has been subsumed here in the wisdom theme of God's dealing with the proud and with the needy (cf.vss.3.9). Now what is the meaning of Isa. liv 1b? Is Israel's new felicity compared with her former state, before she became desolate? Or is the desolate woman compared in general with the married one in the respect of being prolific in progeny, entirely in line with the experience of the sages who knew that sterility and fertility belong to the realm of the unforeseen, so much so that change of fortune can always come about? In the former sense, the verse announces that the present bereavement of the threshed Israel will yield to a fertility which surpasses that of her former state, when she was still married to God. Although the prophets are accustomed to compare the new salvation with the old time of grace, this kind of statement is beside the question in the context. Moreover, in that case the wisdom character of the sentence would be sheer form, the content itself being not a general truth but an announcement of salvation. Since, as we have seen above, the wisdom tradition has integrated the historical topic of God's intervention on behalf of sterile women, we are inclined to interpret Isa. liv 1b in the latter sense. The verse points out to the desolate woman the experience which stems from the vicissitudes of some married women in Israel's history. Beyond the experience lies God's intervention in human life. Although that intervention is not mentioned, it is clear that the statement does not apply to any desolate and any married woman, but to some particular women, objects of God's care. It does not apply within the commonness of human experience, but in the realm of God's dealing with Israel to the extent that his pity for barren women is a recurrent phenomenon, an experience of the faithful community.

Thus, the motivation for rejoicing is at the same time experience and promise. God reminds Israel of what can be observed in the life of desolate women. Actually he points back to all those women in the past who have met with God's mercy. Sarah, the first of them, and the other matriarchs are, of course, the main point of reference. The very fact that he calls to mind what eventually is due to his own action, makes the experience into a promise. In the present Israel the vicissitude of Sarah and the others will be repeated.

4. The imagery of the woman who must enlarge the place of her tent (2) is akin, first to Isa. xlix 19 ff., where the same promise is applied to Zion, and next to Jer. x 19 f., a communal lament, by which the people [1]), represented as a mother (20 : 'my children'), answers to God's announcing an imminent exile. With regard to the two passages of DI, WESTERMANN has positively pointed to the age-old lament of the childless woman as their basic literary pattern [2]). Subsequently, CRÜSEMANN has brought forward the thesis that the literary form of the summons to rejoice, which is mostly addressed to a woman representing either a country or a city [3]), does not stem from the hymn. It rather constitutes a prophetic expression of encouragement tracing its origin to the oracle of salvation which replies to the sterile woman's lament. In no text is this original Sitz-im-Leben more perceptible than in Isa. liv 1. Thus, the original literary genre (cf. Gen. xxv 21 : Rebekah) has been applied to the people when it came to be bereft of its children because of whatever calamity, for, of old, the collectivity was symbolized as woman and mother. The book of Lamentations bears witness to this transfer of use (i 1.5.20). The text of Jer. x 19 f. mentioned above points in the same direction and seems, moreover, to suggest that the metaphorical language of setting up the tent belongs to the furnishing of that literary genre. As the childless woman wails over her loneliness in the tent, so the mother bereft of her children complains that she has none to put up her tent. The abandoned mother, however, to whom the prophet addresses his oracle of salvation, will have to enlarge her tent-space in order to make room for her children. The image changes as the situation of the woman Israel changes,

---

[1]) So W. RUDOLPH, *Jeremia* (HAT), Tübingen 1968[3], p. 75.—J. M. BERRIDGE, *Prophet, People and the Word of Yahweh* (Basel Stud. of Theol. 4), Zürich 1970, p. 176, explains the passage so that the prophet is speaking here, "thereby disclosing the oneness which he knows with his people", but he does not do justice to all the details of the metaphorical language.

[2]) O.c., pp. 179, 219.

[3]) F. CRÜSEMANN, *Studien zur Formgeschichte von Hymnus und Danklied in Israel* (WMANT 32), Neukirchen 1969, pp. 55-65 : Isa. xii 6; liv 1; lxvi 10; Jer. l 11; Zeph. iii 14 f; Zech. ii 14; ix 9 f.; Lam. iv 21; (Isa. xiv 29; Hos. ix 1; Jo. ii 21-24; Mi. vii 8).

whether ancestress or people, before God. The lament itself does not change, its continuity bears history. It would involve a rationalsitic approach to our text to deny that the reality of lamenting through the ages, bound to its own patterns and metaphors, links up Sarah and the bereft Israel. After all, Sarah was in the tent when the Lord said to Abraham : "I will surely return to you in the spring and Sarah your wife shall have a son" (Gen. xviii 9 [1]). As JONES commenting the DI passage has put it : "The tent of the mother of Israel is the sign of her station" [2]).

We shall pass now to the second section, in which the prophet addresses himself to the woman as the abandoned wife of Yhwh. Since this other image is fully elaborated, we are in no need of a clear proof for the influence of that old prophetic tradition which had started with Hosea and was carried on by Jeremiah and Ezechiel. We shall confine ourselves to elaborating a few less obvious matters.

What strikes the eye is that the build-up of the second section forms the counterpart of the first half. "Fear not" (4) is the reverse of "rejoice" (1), the promise that she will again enjoy the alliance of married life (5) corresponds to the assertion that she will have to enlarge her tent-space for her new breed (2f.). Finally, God's motivations (1b.6b) for changing the mood of distress and fear into one of joy and courage open and close the prophet's speech.

We may touch upon the kernel of the address by raising a question that is generally overlooked by commentators : what is the subject and what is the predicate in the two nominal sentences of vs.5 : *kî bō'ălayik 'ōśayik* and *w^egō'ălēk q^edôš yiśrā'ēl*? From the translations we do not gain insight into how tranlators interpret these lines because in modern languages it is not the word-sequence which is decisive but the context and intonation. The one author who has dealt with this problem is KÖHLER [3]). After stating that the regular syntactical sequence in Hebrew is first the predicate, then the subject, he shows that this rule holds good also for DI. Then he lists the instances in which the subject precedes the predicate, according to the various effects which ensue from

---

[1]) How important the tent of Sarah has become in the biblical tradition, can be discovered from Gen. xxiv 67, where either the narrator or the later transmitter tells that Isaac brought Rebekah into the tent of Sarah his mother. As for the textual problems of this verse, cf. the commentaries.

[2]) D. R. JONES, "Isaiah II and III", in : *Peake's Commentary on the Bible*, London 1963[2], p. 528.

[3]) O.c., pp. 58-66, esp. p. 64.

the inversion. The verse which is at stakes here, we find classified under those *kî*-sentences which display the natural sequence. Arguments, however, in support of this case are not adduced. So, in his view, *bō'ălayik* and *gō'ălēk* are predicate, *'ōśayik* and *qᵉdôš yiśrā'ēl* are subject. This may be the interpretation of the RSV too for this translation has changed the sequence of the words as compared to the Hebrew version : "For your Maker is your husband... and the Holy One of Israel is your Redeemer". We can paraphrase this choice as follows : "Your Maker is your husband, he marries you" and set it against the opposite interpretation (rejected by KÖHLER) : "Your husband is your Maker, he has created you".

Now, are we forced to agree with the interpretation of KÖHLER ? I think in first instance that we are. The context does not support the opposite interpretation, It would be illogical to point out to the woman who has just been called unmarried and widow (4) the unique qualities of her husband and her kinsman. On the other hand, it is perfectly in keeping with the preceding encouragement to announce to this same woman that someone, in this case her Maker, will marry her, that the Holy One of Israel will act as her kinsman.—The same can be argued from the point of view of form-criticism. We saw above (p. 36, note 1) that the structure of these three verses makes a perfect example of the classic oracle of salvation. Now, vs. 5 forms the first part (the nominal sentence) of the so-called *Begründung*, the reason for encouragement, which itself announces God's intervention. In other words, according to the pattern of the literary genre concerned, we are told here what God will do for the afflicted woman, not who the person is that will perform the saving intervention.

However much we agree with KÖHLER 's choice, this should not result in our regarding the subject of these sentences, i.e. your Maker and the Holy One of Israel, as self-evident data, that element on which speaker and person addressed agree, the entity which, as far as it is determined in itself, holds no surprise, the surprise being only the predicate, i.e. what will be stated about it. The two words by which the subject is defined, *'ōśayik* and *qᵉdôš yiśrā'ēl*, are, to some degree, predicative as well : not from the syntactic point of view but in terms of the message to be conveyed. The prophet calls God by these names precisely because he wants to proclaim that he is Creator and the Holy One of Israel. These qualities of the subject of his statement warrant the reliability of that statement. Because he is the Creator of Israel he will be her husband, because he is her Holy One the fact that he will act as her kinsman merits her belief. It would take us too far afield to describe fully the impact of these attributes upon the passage at issue. Suffice it to say with regard to the verb *'śh* in DI that "by far the largest number of occurrences (20 × out of 23 ×) regard Yahweh's *making* Israel or Zion or *doing* for her" [1]). Concerning the attribute 'the Holy One of Israel' we refer to ELLIGER's summarizing remark that with DI, as opposed to the first Isaiah, the accent is on Israel: "Der Heilige ist trotz allem, was inzwischen geschehen ist, Israels Gott, der unverrückt das Heil seines Volkes im Auge hat" [2]). Neither term has been chosen haphazardly. They constitute motif-words that bear the concept of God's alliance to Israel: both his creative activity and his distinctness aim at Israel's felicity [3]).

The foregoing leads us to another consideration. Recent studies (especially of WESTERMANN [4])) have elucidated the differences of origin, form and tendency between the oracle of salvation (Heilsorakel) and the announcement of salvation (Heilsankündigung). The basic

---

[1]) STUHLMUELLER, o.c., pp. 218, cf. 216 ff.

[2]) K. ELLIGER, *Jesaja II* (BK), Neukirchen 1970-, p. 152.

[3]) The question we raised here has to do with the relation between creation and redemption in DI. The same topic has been broached by H.-J. HERMISSON from a different point of view in: "Diskussionsworte bei Deuterojesaja", *EvTh* 31 (1971), pp. 665-680. He contests the quite common understanding according to which DI could expect his audience to believe in God's creative power so that he only had to lead his people from there to hoping for a divine intervention in their historical situation: "Haben wir die Texte richtig verstanden, so steht die Krise jener Zeitgenossen des Propheten neueren Glaubenskrisen nicht mehr so fern. Es waren dann nicht Menschen, deren Glauben an Jahwe den Schöpfer unerschüttert geblieben war, und die insofern mit einer weit besseren religiösen Konstitution ausgestattet waren. Gewiss: der Prophet konnte verschüttete Traditionen wieder aufdecken, aber dass er diese Traditionen wieder aufnimmt, hat viel mehr theologische als pädagogische Gründe; und dass jene Tradition die Erfahrung des Glaubens, den Reichtum des Glaubens Israels repräsentierte—einen Reichtum, an dem auch diese unglückliche Generation noch teilhaben sollte—, das galt es erst wieder evident zu machen... Er hat ihre religiösen Zweifel, ihre aktuellen Fragen ernst genommen, und er hat die Antwort darauf gegeben, indem er sie in den grösseren theologischen Horizont des Schöpfungsglaubens eingeordnet hat" (conclusion, p. 680).

[4]) Cf. WESTERMANN's studies mentioned on p. 36, note 1, and the summary in his commentary, o.c., pp. 13-16. The distinction between oracle of salvation and announcement of salvation has wrongly been rejected by J. SCHÜPPHAUS, "Stellung und Funktion der sogenannten Heilsankündigung bei Deuterojesaja", *ThZ* 27 (1971), pp. 161-181. It is true that these literary genres seldom occur in DI in their original pure structure and as independent unities. As different forms of speech, however, integrated into larger compositions and freely used according to the actual situation and the creative literary genius of the prophet, they can easily be discerned.

discrepancy is in this : the oracle places the deliverance present in the life of the suppliant; the perfect tense is its characteristic, the perfect of the decision that has already been made by God and is working therefore in the situation of distress. On the other hand, the announcement is essentially future, it proclaims what will happen in the new era to be inaugurated by God's intervention. For all the remodelling that the basic pattern has undergone in the wife-section of our chapter, the fundamental time-aspect of the literary genre of the oracle of salvation should be kept in sight. The tenor is one of present salvation : in the distance the rescuer enters on the scene, the husband is announced as coming to take away the solitude of the abandoned wife. The very fact that vss.4-6 present the structure of an oracle of salvation while lacking the characteristic element of God's speaking in the first person, raises the demand for his personal appearance. In this way, the direct address of God in the second part of the chapter is prepared.

A final remark has to do with the two phrases that conclude the two halves of vs.5 : "The Lord of host is his name" and "The God of the whole earth he is called". CRENSHAW investigated the first expression and arrived at the conclusion that it is a doxological formula, which has come into practice in the exilic community [1]). The second expression (...*yiqqārē'*) occurs several times in order to proclaim solemnly someone's first or new name [2]). Though the latter has no cultic connotation of its own, it is given a cultic function here as it stands parallel to the former. These doxologies are in no way an erratic block within this context. As we have seen, 'your Maker' and 'the Holy One of Israel' are not only subject but somehow predicative as well. So, the qualifications of God contained in these attributes pave the way to an exclamatory line, single words open out into sentences, proclamation of rescue ends in confession and praise. Within the oracle of salvation God's powerful names are exclaimed to the suppliant. The proclamation of God's salvific presence to the afflicted appellant is followed by the confession of what he is like. The lament of the woman is met by

---

1) Cf. J. L. CRENSHAW, "*YHWH Ṣebā'ôt Šemô*" : a Form-Critical Analysis", *ZAW* 81 (1969), pp. 156-176.—Isa. liv 5 should be classified with the first group of literary employment ('dangling modifier') rather than with the third subdivision of the second group ('formula plus lengthy sentence ': pp. 165 f.).

2) With *šēm* : Gen. xvii 5; xxxv 10; Isa. iv 26; without *šēm* : Gen. ii 23; Isa. i 26; xxxv 8; liv 5; lxii 4. 12; Jer. xix 6.

the appraisal of God [1]). Only against the horizon of God's might it can be surmised that his rescue is imminent. At the same time the rescue to come ushers in the praise of his sovereignty. The extent to which the praise widens the outlook of the dirge, is displayed by the climactic sequence of divine epithets in this verse. The Holy One, who has pledged himself to Israel, is the God of the whole earth, the Maker of Israel is the Lord who has brought out the host of heaven (cf. xl 26; xlv 12).

In summary : the appeal of the prophet addresses a nameless woman in the twofold shape of the barren ancestress Sarah and the forsaken wife. This double identity tallies with the two phases of Israel's history up to the exile. Two female images, which in Israel's traditions occupy a place special enough to symbolize its past existence, endow the woman with their features. However, the person addressed is not a figure from antiquity. It is the actual people of the exilic epoch represented by the symbols of the former times. Israel is identified with its past in order to foreshadow the new era of prolificity and God's everlasting love.

2. *The discourse of God* (*7-17*)

The prophet's appeal is followed by an address of God, which itself consists of two quite distinct parts. Previously we have seen that they ought not be separated as independent unities. To the formal arguments in favour of their coherence given above the subsequent thematic discussion may be added.

a. *God's message transmitted by the prophet* (*7-10*)

At first glance there seems to be no need of dealing with the first section since it only gives a portrayal of God whereas we have made it our task to inquire after the multiple identity of the woman addressed. However, the portraying of God is all done in terms of the husband who has compassion on the woman whom he left in anger : *'zb* (6f.) clearly forms the catch-word of the two parts of the chapter. So, this description really adds to the picture of the woman spoken to. From this point of view, we shall investigate these verses.

The messenger formulae not only characterize the whole section as God's tidings proclaimed by the prophet (see above), but at the same time they mark the twofold structure of this small unity : in vss.7 f.

---

1) It is one of the great merits of WESTERMANN's commentary that he has elucidated the form-critical and theological connection between lament and hymn within Isa. xl-lv.

God announces his everlasting fidelity, in vss.9 f. he confirms his promise by means of an oath which draws a parallel with his covenant with Noah. Finally, the divine epithets which are incorporated into the formulae have a specific function : the first one, *gō'ălēk* (8), is the middelmost of the three predicates of God announced in vss.5 f.; the second, *m^erahămēk* (10), takes up the important (because enclosing) term for God's mercy of vss.7 f.

A survey of the manifold use of parallelism (synonymous, antithetic and ascending) in this passage is most instructive. As for vss.7 f. the antithetic parallelism of the two halves of each verse is clear : 7a//7b; 8aα//8aβ. There is a very ingenious twofold inclusion of interlocking disposition : the first halves of these verses dealing with the woman's past forlornness (7a.8aα) are enclosed by the word *rega'*, the second halves (7b.8aβ) announcing God's new love are enclosed by words belonging to the root *rḥm*.

The *rega'*-inclusion opens a line of *b*e-adjuncts, which by way of ascending parallelism leads to the word that is in the focus of the passage : *'ôlām* :

7a *b^erega' qāṭōn*
7b *ûb^eraḥămîm g^edōlîm*
8aα *b^ešeṣep qeṣep... rega'*
8aβ *ûb^eḥesed 'ôlām*

rega' itself although basicly a category of time "evokes specific bad associations" [1]). Characteristic words denoting calamity, wrath etc. are apt to recur in the context of this term [2]). It is striking that in the parallel member of vs.7a an antithetic concept of time does not occur : only the aspect of wrath contained in *rega'* is met by the word *raḥămîm*. The next adjunct (8aα) likewise omits the aspect of time and fully elaborates the other aspect (*b^ešeṣep qeṣep* [3])). Then, however, in the next part of the first half-verse the neglect is recovered by the same

---

1) N. J. TROMP, *Primitive Conceptions of Death and the Nether World in the Old Testament*, (Bibl. Or. 21), Rome 1969, pp. 81 ff.

2) D. DAUBE, *The Sudden in the Scriptures*, Leiden 1964, pp. 9 ff.—This is the case in almost all the instances of the word : Ex. xxxiii 5; Num. xvi 21; xvii 10; Isa. xxvi 20; xlvii 9; liv 7 f.; Jer. iv 20; xviii 7.9; Ez. xxvi 16; xxxii 10; Ps. vi 11; xxx 6; lxxiii 19; Job vii 18; xx 5; xxi 13; xxxiv 20; Lam. iv 6; exceptions : Isa. xxvii 3; Ezra ix 8.

3) *qṣp* is used by DI only for God's anger towards Israel : xlvii 6; liv 8 f. The same holds good for Trito-Isaiah : lvii 16 f.; lx 10; lxiv 4.8.

word *rega'*, now merely in the sense of 'moment'. Thus the time aspect of God's dealing with Israel is stressed : this prepares for the word that constitutes part of the climax : *'ôlām*.

Likewise, there is a progress leading to the other word of the climax : *ḥesed*. The element of God's mood towards Israel is implicitly contained in the first *rega'*, is fully expressed by *raḥămîm*, then by *šeṣep qeṣep* and finally by *ḥesed*. This word forms the climax because *riḥamtîk* brings nothing new or surprising. So, in *ḥesed 'ôlām* the promise really reaches its climax : "With everlasting fidelity I will have compassion on you". It is the same two words which provoke the comparison with the oath to Noah contained in the next two verses : "As I swore that the waters of Noah should *no more* go over the earth", and "My *fidelity* shall not depart...".

The verbs that occur in vss.7f. are not less interesting in their position determined by the parallelism. *'ăzabtîk*—the word that links this passage with the previous one (6)— is met in contrast by *'ăqabbeṣēk*. *qbṣ* has a twofold meaning in DI : a forensic one, 'to assemble sc. in court' [1]) and 'to gather from exile' [2]). The latter must be supposed here [3]). So, *qbṣ* in antithetic parallelism to *'zb* adds an important trait to the picture of the woman. Her loneliness consists of her dispersion into exile. Thus, whereas the prophetic appeal has not explained the image of Israel's forlornness (4 ff.), but rather continued the figure of the desolate land of Israel (evoked by the summons that the deserted mother enlarge her tent-space and by the promise that her seed will people desolate cities [1 ff.]), the speech of God from the outset focuses on the other aspect of Israel's misfortune : her distorted existence in exile. This application of the image of being deserted draws on the line of Israel's history. Since God left his wife, Israel consists of two popu-

---

1) Nif. : xliii 9; xlv 20; xlviii 14; hitp. : xliv 11.

2) Nif. : xlix 18; pi. : xl 11; xliii 5; liv 7.

3) NBG apparently understands *'ăqabbeṣēk* wholly in function of its parallel member *'ăzabtîk* : "Ik zal u tot Mij nemen". Likewise NAB : "I will take you back" and maybe PB : "Ich führe dich heim" and NEB : "I will bring you home". Among the commentators R. Kittel, o.c., p. 464 : "*Ich werde dich an mich ziehen...* kraft des Gegensatzes". —It is, however, not a sound procedure to determine the content of a word from its position within the parallelism in such a way that its normal meaning in this particular book and in the whole of the O.T. is given up. *qbṣ* nowhere means 'to take a person back'. Here the regular sense of 'to gather from exile' rather stands in tension with the aspect imparted by the parallel *'ăzabtîk* : the gathering of Israel is somehow a gathering around God, her husband.

lation groups, one in the home-land, one in dispersion, both afflicted and in miserable condition. This twofold manifestation of the one Israel will occupy us more later.—The next verb in parallelism returns from the application to the image and again announces God's change of mood towards Israel. For a while, he has hidden his face from the woman, he has prevented himself from seeing the miserable condition of his wife [1]) and not let his life giving face be a bliss for Israel. From now on, he will turn to the woman and have compassion on her with everlasting fidelity.

Thus, the first two lines of God's address develop the preceding announcement : the contrast of the bygone distress and the new felicity proclaimed there by the prophet is now explained by God himself as a change of attitude towards her. God hands over the key to understanding the way he has made her go : for a moment he has been angry, with everlasting fidelity he will love her. This pair of terms discloses the future of the woman. At the same time her present situation, the exile, is mentioned.

Vss.9 f. elaborate the promise of God's everlasting fidelity in a comparison (9), which carries with it a second antithetic comparison which develops the first one (10). It is to be asked : how are these verses related to each other ?

The answer depends primarily on how we understand *kî* in vs.10 : causal [2]) or concessive [3]). The former interpretation seems inconvenient because vs.10 does not contain the motivation of vs.9, but rather its climax. The latter sense is certainly involved in the meaning and structure of the verse, even apart from the particle itself [4]). We would like to argue, however, for an emphatic function of *kî*. This meaning does not derogate from the concessive tenor of the first stichos, but strengthens it. It would be more in line with the climactic character of vs.10 vis-a-vis vs.9. In this way, vs.10 may be understood as the content of the oath that Yhwh announces in the previous verse : "Verily, the mountains may depart... but my fidelity shall not depart from you".

---

[1]) Cf. J. Reindl, *Das Angesicht Gottes im Sprachgebrauch des Alten Testaments* (Erfurter Theol. Stud. 25), Leipzig 1970, pp. 89-109.

[2]) NBG, RSV, ZB, PB, BJ, North, McKenzie, Westermann; P. A. H. de Boer, *Second-Isaiah's Message* (OTSt XI), Leiden 1956.

[3]) NEB, NAB, Delitzsch, Duhm.

[4]) Cf. Th. C. Vriezen, "Einige Notizen zur Übersetzung des Bindewortes *kî*" in: *Von Ugarit nach Qumran* (BZAW 77), Berlin 1958, pp. 266-273.

In view of this we should not omit pointing to the perfect tense of *nišba'tî* in vs.9b : this cannot but be the characteristic tense of that part of the oracle of salvation which is called *Begründung* (see p. 36, note 1). It is now that God's oath becomes salvific reality in the life of Israel. Then, the imperfect *lō'-yāmûš* in vs.10 marks the *Folge* of the oracle of salvation. So, from the form-critical point of view vs.9 and vs.10 are interrelated as two elements of the oracle of salvation, i.e. as reason (verbal sentence, perfect tense) and result (imperfect). This structure, however, is not the dominant one. It serves the prevailing build-up of announcement of oath and the oath itself. So too, the concluding messenger formula appears to full adventage.

Also with regard to the content of the passage vs.10b must be seen as its peak : it continues the topic of 'for a moment—for ever' of vss.7 f. As we remarked, *'ôd* (in connection with *mē'ăbōr*) in vs.9 takes up the chief concept of vs.8: *ḥesed 'ôlām*. Now, it is immediately apparent that *'ôd* has no parallel word in the next stichos (instead *ûmiggeʿor-bāk* is found). The lack is supplied for by a whole verse which makes its point of the never-failing character of God's fidelity. *weḥasdî mē'ittēk lō'-yāmûš* (10) is an amplification of *beḥesed 'ôlām* (8). Thus the same literary device we discovered in vss.7 f. is used here in order to shed full light on the message that God's love will never fall back again.

What do these verses add to the image of the woman? First, the everlasting character of God's fidelity is confirmed by an oath. Then, her new felicity receives the steadfastness of the Noachic covenant. We must take the comparison with God's oath to Noah as seriously as a Semitic comparison is intended to be : the model is not a didactic or kerygmatic example, but something that communicates its reality to that with which it is compared. In the realm of history, as is the case here, a comparison is paramount to an actualization [1]). As God acted in the old days, so he intervenes now in the destiny of men and peoples. The values which are associated with the typos, become new reality in the antitypos.

The introductory words of vs.9 already confirm what we just said, if, as we presume [2]), they are to be read as *kîmê* : "Like the days

---

[1]) As for these questions, see G. von Rad, *Theologie des Alten Testaments II*, München 1965[4], pp. 342-349 ("inneralttestamentliche Neuinterpretationen").

[2]) The text-critical evidence can be read in the apparatus of BHK[3]. D. W. Thomas in BHS prefers the reading of the LXX : "Like the waters of Noah is this to me" (so earlier Delitzsch and Buber). The interpretation 'days' is accepted by all the translations that we in this article usually consult and by the majority of the commentators.

of Noah is this to me". Thus a comparison of epochs is meant here [1]). The days of Noah have returned in the present change from distress to bliss. What that period entailed for the order of the world, i.e. steadfastness, is at the present time becoming the inalienable good of Israel.

From the literary point of view this is expressed by the parallel position of *'al-hā'āreṣ* and *'ālayik* (*...bāk*) in vs.9. The simile is quite bold : can the firmness of the natural order be compared with the measure of security that is the outlook of this afflicted woman who represents a tiny people? The comparison is unmistakable though. Israel is not set side by side with Noah, 'the righteous man, blameless in his generation' (Gen. vi 9), but with the earth. There had been no righteousness at all in Israel: she was the object of God's anger and rage [2]). While *mē'ăbōr mê-nōaḥ 'ôd 'al-hā'āreṣ* does not imply that the earth itself had sinned, the parallel verbs *miqqeṣōp 'ālayik ûmiggeʻor-bāk* certainly suggest that Israel had provoked God's wrath by her conduct. This difference modifies the parallelism which connects 'the earth' and 'you', i.e. Israel, but does not dissolve it. Long ago the earth escaped doom and gained a stability that it will never lose. Now this people has escaped its total ruin and gained God's fidelity, which will never depart from it. The new trait added to the image of the woman consists of her likeness to the earth : neither will collapse since God's oath warrants their existence. We are tempted to say : Israel is sketched here in terms of creation restituted [3]).

The impact of the concurrent position of the earth and Israel can further be developped since we know, thanks to the research of VAN DER MERWE, that DI stands more in the priestly tradition of the deluge story than in the yahwistic one (although it is out of the question that the prophet was familiar with the priestly narrative in its present state) [4]). One cannot help being reminded of the fact that the priestly tradition strongly emphasizes the coherence of man's behaviour and

---

1) Cf. DELITZSCH, o.c., p. 536; DE BOER, o.c., p. 56.

2) *g'r* means 'the physical expression of anger', rather than 'to rebuke' with the connotation of moral reprimand. "When God is the subject, its connotation is both his anger and the effective working out of his anger": A. A. MACINTOSH, "A Consideration of Hebrew *g'r*", *VT* 19 (1969), pp. 471-479 (summary p. 479). Our text is not mentioned in this study.

3) It goes without saying that here we touch upon a field of major interest in the prophecies of DI, cf. STUHLMUELLER, o.c.

4) O.c., pp. 74-89.

the destiny of earth. McEVENUE has brought to our notice the palistrophe by which P opens his account of the flood narrative after the introductory *tôlᵉdōt* of Noah (Gen. vi 11-13) [1]). The palistrophe hinges on the words *hā'āreṣ*, *kol-bāśār* and the root *šḥt*. So, from the very beginning the relation between earth and its inhabitants is under discussion, so much so that it bears a figure of speech, and this cannot be said of the yahwistic story (Gen. vi 5-8). In the first speech of God out of three that conclude P's narrative (Gen. ix 1-7. 8-11.12-17), the blessing on the first man (Gen. i 28) is renewed on Noah and his sons in such a way that it includes the speech : "Be fruitful and multiply and fill the earth//And you, be fruitful and multiply, bring forth abundantly on the earth and multiply in it" (Gen. ix 1.7) [2]). Obviously, the same topic of man on earth is repeated here. The second speech of God, which contains his oath, harks back to the triplet of *kol-bāśār*, *šḥt* and *hā-'āreṣ* (Gen. ix 11) and, moreover, it contains the word *'ôd* twice, which, as we have seen, is of no little importance in Isa. liv 9. The third speech, which deals with the rainbow, the sign of the oath, concludes again with the theme of *kol-bāśār 'ăšer 'al-hā'āreṣ* (Gen. ix 17). It is evident that in the P-story of the deluge the theme 'man on earth' has inspired several literary forms of speech.

Seen against this background the concurrent position of 'earth' and 'you' in Isa. liv 9 gains new light. The parallelism does not leave the earth and Israel in splendid isolation, God's fidelity relates them to each other. This earth firm as a rock since God's oath to Noah is to be the abode of this woman, who since God's new oath enjoys his unquenchable love. From now on, the possession of an indestructible living ground belongs to the portrayal of the woman. She can no longer be thought of but as dwelling on a place which no power will ever capture. It will be obvious that this theme prepares the next section (11-17) in many ways.

Finally a few remarks concerning vs.10. We have seen that it constitutes the climax of the passage because it apparently mentions the content of God's oath to the woman, in which he elaborates the adjunct *bᵉḥesed 'ôlām* (8) into a full statement. The comparison continues the creation context, which the previous verse had introduced by the concept of the earth and all what is associated with it. The oath closes with

---

[1]) S. McEVENUE, *The Narrative Style of the Priestly Writer* (An. Bibl. 50), Rome 1971, pp. 28 ff.

[2]) Ibd., pp. 67-71.

a word not used in this chapter before in which the exposition reaches its climax : "My covenant of peace shall not totter". In *b^e^rît š^e^lômî* the line that began with *raḥămîm* (7) and passed by *ḥesed 'ôlām* (8) has reached its peak. It is well-known that especially this term is the ground for connecting DI's reference to the flood narrative with the priestly tradition, rather than with the yahwistic story, in which *b^e^rît* does not occur [1]). Gen. ix 16 reads : "When the bow is in the clouds, I will look upon it and remember the everlasting covenant (*b^e^rît 'ôlām*) between God and every living creature of all flesh that is upon earth". By 'the covenant of peace which shall not totter' DI recapitulates what has been said in this first part of God's speech : it is the woman Israel who will enjoy the unperturbed peace of God's fidelity on an earth that likewise will never again be jeopardized by the outburst of God's anger [2]). Above we have stated that the comparison functions as an actualization. After the foregoing discussion we are allowed to give that statement more weight by pointing out to a remark of VRIEZEN : what DI sees happening is "*the* renewing act of *the* historical drama... it takes place within the historical frame of the world, but it is something that definitely changes this world" [3]). Now that earth *and* people of God will be rooted in his everlasting fidelity, the world is about to find its final shape.

b. *The personal allocution of God (11-17)*

The previous section contained God's declaration of everlasting love transmitted by the prophet. Now he calls upon the woman personally.

---

[1]) VAN DER MERWE, o.c., pp. 79 ff.

[2]) The comparison (10) certainly does not mean that the mountains as opposed to God's fidelity will totter (pace BEGRICH, o.c., p. 83). In my view, the verse must be seen as a 'dialectic negation'. As to this form of speech, cf. H. KRUSE, "Die 'Dialektische Negation' als Semitisches Idiom", *VT* 4 (1954), pp. 385-400. KRUSE discusses the locution 'not A, but B' and explains it as meaning 'not so much A as B'. Vs. 10 seems to represent a variant of the same literary phenomenon : 'A, notB', which may mean 'suppose A, not B'. Applied to our verse this results in : "In case the mountains totter, my fidelity will not totter". The image of the comparison is not adduced as a reality but as a possibility (cf. Ps. xlvi 3) or as an irreal supposition. The latter may hold good here (cf. DUHM, o.c., p. 410) because God's oath regarding the stability of the earth seems to involve the firmness of the mountains. Cf. the problem of the exegesis of Mt. xxiv 35.

[3]) Th. C. VRIEZEN, "Prophecy and Eschatology", in : *Congress Volume Copenhagen* 1953 (Suppl. VT 1), Leiden 1953, p. 218.

This second section of God's message opens with a threefold address: "O afflicted one, tempest-driven [1]), and not comforted" (11). If we consider vss.11-17 as an independent unity, its opening might be called "abrupt, without introductory formula" [2]) or anything like that [3]). These remarks, however, do not stand since we have come to see that a personal allocution of God functions well as the finale of the chapter. The triple address is in line with the threefold summons by which the prophet opens his appeal (1) and with the triplet of characteristics for the woman and for God in the wife-section (4 ff.). Moreover, we have admitted that the perfect *q^erā'āk* (6) should be understood as presentic: God is *now* calling his forsaken wife. It seems reasonable to interpret vs.11a as the fulfilment of that oracle of salvation. First God issued a statement about his new love for Israel (7-10). Now he actually calls her. Vs.11, by which he does so, "returns characteristically to vs.1, both in the person addressed and in the motif of reversal" [4]).

The three epithets of the new address add some new features to the potrayal of the woman. DI uses the root *'ny* first for the *affliction* of the exile: "I have tried you in the furnace of affliction" (xlviii 10). By means of the word 'furnace' he interprets the sojourn in Babylon as a new Egypt [5]). As God led Israel out of Egypt, so he will lead his afflicted ones out of that land of affliction (xli 17; xlix 13). The word is applied secondly to Zion, the mother bereft of her children (li 21). So both the people in exile and the devastated homeland qualify for the epithet 'afflicted' [6]). The woman represents the two groups of Israel's population.—The last of the three appellatives, 'not comforted' [7]), points in the same direction. DI announces God's comfort (*nḥm*) as well to the

---

1) 'Tempest-driven' seems to be a better translation than 'storm-tossed' (RSV), which "is too suggestive of a storm at sea" (North, o.c.,p. 252).

2) North, o.c., p. 251.

3) Westermann, o.c., p. 223.

4) J. Muilenburg, "Isaiah Ch. 40-66", in: *The Interpreter's Bible* V, New York 1956, p. 638.

5) *kûr* is used for Egypt in Deut. iv 20; 1 Ki. viii 51; Jer. xi 4.

6) Moreover, the nif'al and pu'al of the root are applied to the Servant (liii 4.7).

7) It cannot be denied that *lō' nuḥāmâ* may allude to the second child of Hosea, called *lō' ruḥāmâ* (Hos. i 6; ii 25), who symbolized that God would no more have pity on the house of Israel (so Fischer, o.c., p. 143). It is evident that DI was acquainted with the Hosean tradition of the abandoned wife. The choice of *lō' nuḥāmâ* may have been inspired by the desire to introduce the important topic of the comfort of Israel (see next footnote). Moreover, *lō' ruḥāmâ* would collide with the preceding *m^eraḥămēk* (10).

gôlâ (xlix 13; li 12) as to Jerusalem (li 3.19) [1]).—The middle appellative, 'tempest-driven', is not used with regard to Israel elsewhere, but to her opponents: 'the rulers of the earth' (xl 24) and 'the mountains and hills' (xli 16) [2]) will be taken away by the tempest. This noun (*seʿārâ*) connotes in DI God's judgement, which makes peoples vanish. Its occurrence in Isa. liv 11 points neither to the exiles nor to the homeland specificly. It marks the woman as struck by God's judgement to such a degree that she was about to be scattered without trace.—So taken together the three epithets describe a situation which is that of the present Israel. Living a divided existence in exile and the homeland she is on the verge of vanishing under God's judgement and devoid of his comfort [3]).

Next the structure of this section must be the topic of discussion. Since I have advocated and demonstrated, as I hope, the intrinsic unity of the chapter, we can dismiss those explanations that divide the section into independent unities merely on grounds of the content [4]) or the "level of expression and poetry" [5]). What, however, is the build-up of these verses? We have seen the importance of the twofold *hinnēh* (11b.16): this word emphasizes God's presence with the woman, the predominant topic of the chapter, from which its total structure ensues. Yet, this term does not mark the opening of two subdivisions, for in both cases a call upon the woman in distress and fright precedes (11a and 14b.15). Then the question arises: does vs.14a belong to the first part or the second? I think it can conveniently be considered as the 'hinge-verse': on the one hand it continues the topic of the new city to be founded (11-13), on the other hand the word *ṣedāqâ* encloses the second element of this section (14-17). Moreover, the asyndese of vs.14 marks a new beginning.

[1]) In two other instances the object of God's comfort is 'my/this people' (xl 1; lii 9). In both texts 'people' stands parallel to 'Jerusalem'. It is not evident that this parallelism is sheerly synonymous. It may be that 'people' is used here in an all-embracing sense so that it comes to mean the whole people, those in exile as well as those at home. That would suit the opening line of the book (xl 1) and the context of the other verse (lii 9).—In DI *ʿam* refers to the exiles (xliii 8.20 f.; xlix 13; lii 5 f.), to Zion (li 16.22), to Jacob/Israel (xlii 22, cf. 24) and to Israel as a whole (xl 7; xlii 6; xliv 7; xlvii 6; xlix 8; li 4.7; lii 4; liii 8).

[2]) What 'the mountains and the hills' exactly stands for, is under discussion; cf. the commentaries.

[3]) There is no need of changing vs. 11a into *ʿăniyyâ šeʿārêhâ leʾên ḥōmâ*, as has been proposed by N. H. Tur-Sinai in *Beth-Mikra* 7 (1962), pp. 85 f.

[4]) Westermann, o.c., p. 223.

[5]) McKenzie, o.c., p. 140.

The unity of the passage can be argued also from its literary genre. STUMMER has drawn attention to the fact that vss.11 f. reflect the influence of the royal building inscriptions in the cuneiform literature [1]). Now it is noticeable how much the whole section resembles the neo-babylonian building-inscriptions in terms of its topics. Of course we should not omit bearing in mind the differences. In the building-inscriptions the king speaks, not God. He relates his pious deeds in favour of this particular monument. First he usually mentions his name and manifold titles, then he may inform us of the ramshackle state in which he found the building, and of his pious intentions to restore it. Either the deity has instructed him to renew the edifice or he has asked the god to accept his building-plans graciously. The inscriptions normally close with a prayer for the preservation of the monument and for bliss on the king and his dynasty [2]). From the point of view of literary genre the contact between Isa. liv 11-17 and those cuneiform building-inscriptions seems to be the following. The Mesopotamian inscriptions presuppose a divine oracle in which the god either commissions the king to build the temple [3]) or favourably accepts his religious projects [4]). God's address to the woman in DI is a building oracle in this sense: God declares that he himself is about to re-establish the city. So the literary genre of our passage is in itself wholly different from the neo-babylonian building-inscriptions. However, they hold a common Sitz-im-Leben: the religious act of founding a public monument. The striking resemblance between Isa. liv 11-17 and those royal inscriptions from Mesopotamia stems from their common socio-religious origin.

This resemblance, then, looks first to the total structure of the passage. WESTERMANN has elucidated that the form of speech of vss. 13b-17 is akin to the blessing (Segenszusage) [5]). Now it seems that

---

[1]) F. STUMMER, "Einige keilschriftliche Parallelen zu Jes. 40-66", *JBL* 45 (1926), pp. 171-189, esp. 188 f.

[2]) Cf. S. LANGDON, *Die neubabylonischen Königsinschriften* (Vorderasiatische Bibliothek 4), Leipzig 1912.—Fast any of the herein published texts answers to our description.

[3]) Ibd., pp. 96 f., col. I, lines (=11) 23-25; pp. 100 f., Nr. 12, 11.22-24; pp. 102 f., 11.16-27.

[4]) Ibd., pp. 62 f., 11.31-33; pp. 238 f., 11.35-39; pp. 246 f.,11.49-51.

[5]) WESTERMANN, o.c., p. 224 : "Die Segenszusage ist von der Heilszusage oder dem Heilsorakel zu unterscheiden : diese ist die Antwort Gottes auf eine Klage und sie sagt die Wende des in ihr geklagten Leides zu; die Segenszusage dagegen sagt das stetige Mitsein, Helfen, Behüten, Segnen Gottes zu. Sie ist nur dieses eine Mal von Deuterojesaja

this second segment forms the counterpart of the prayer for bliss in the royal inscriptions. Below we list a number of topics that occur in both texts :

vs.14a : the firm foundation of the city//throne [1])
vss.14 f : no fear of enemies [2])
vs.17a : weapons will be powerless [3])
vss.17b.(13b) : the well-being of the posterity [4]).

So, against this background of neo-babylonian material it is probable that the blessing segment of this passage, together with the building announcement, forms one subdivision of the chapter, a foundation oracle which God proclaims while he lays the basis of the new city. There is no reason to consider the blessing as an independent unity. What it announces is not a state of well-being that can be expected from any act of salvation. It is the well-being that people hope to gain when a new city is going to be erected : to be far from oppression and fear (14b), the guarantee that possible aggressors wil dash themselves against its walls (15b) and that weapons fashioned against this city will not prosper (17a). In this case the good that is hoped for is all the more unassailable since the city's safety stems from God who is laying its foundations. Therefore, if anyone stirs up strife, it is not from Yhwh (15a) and however strong his weaponry may be made, it is Yhwh who created its smith (16).

Now that we have determined the literary genre and the intrinsic unity of vss.11-17, we raise again the main question which occupies us in this study : how is the woman portrayed here? Evidently, that part of God's message in which he addresses the woman personally switches from the image of the wife to that of the personified city. By means of both the literary genre and the content of this building-oracle the woman addressed assumes the traits of that person who so

---

aufgenommen und auf Israel bezogen, nur hier in Kap. 54, wo es ja durchweg um den Status des Heils geht". —Cf. the following texts : Ps. xci ; xcxxi Job v 17-26. Cf. more specificly Isa. liv 14b with Ps. xci 5a.10; Job. v 9b, and Isa. liv 13b with Job v 25.

[1]) *kânû* (cf. Is. liv 14 : *tikkônānî*) : LANGDON, o.c., pp. 68 f., l.36; pp. 64 f., ll.43-49; pp. 78 f., l.35; pp. 100 f., l.21.

[2]) Ibd., pp. 68 f., ll.33 f.; pp. 84 f., Nr. 5, col. II,ll.23-29; pp. 88 f., Nr. 7,l.31; pp. 120 f., ll.50-53.

[3]) Ibd., pp. 78 f., ll.37-44; pp. 82 f. col. II,l.31; pp. 102 f., col. III,ll.28 f.

[4]) Ibd., pp. 84 f., Nr. 6, col II,ll.12-19; pp. 94 f., ll.49-56; pp. 252 f., col. II,ll.24-31.

often in Hebrew literature represents the people or the city. The daughter of Zion enters on the scene, the feminine collective representation, the woman who embodies the spirit, history and destiny of its inhabitants.

We should notice, however, that her name is not mentioned. This remarkable omission produces several effects. First of all, it parallels the fact that the names of Sarah and Israel do not occur in the prophet's appeal. Because these three names are missing, the one identity of the woman under her several shapes is safeguarded. Mother, wife and city : the picture of the woman is complete now. How these three images are linked up, is a question that we shall deal with in the next part of this study.

Another effect which ensues from the absence of the name Zion is the following. We have seen that the address of vs.11a ("O afflicted one, tempest-driven, and not comforted") involves a conscious attempt to call upon the woman Israel in her divided existence, an attempt to gather in this summons both the group in the homeland and that in exile. Mentioning the name Zion right after this refined address would take away its meaning. Now the double greeting is continued to the effect that the woman spoken to is more than the Zion which lives a miserable existence upon the ruins of the old city. She is also the Zion with which the miserable exiles identify themselves and to which they fervently want to return. The new Zion for which God is now laying the foundations will comprise both populations within its walls.

In order to have our exegesis of vss.11-17 confirmed we should describe the intrinsic relations which connect this section with the rest of the chapter. In spite of the fact that commentaries have habitually neglected them—probably because they are neither obvious nor bound to motif-words—, we consider them very real. They are part of the new content of this address.

To begin with, we shall look for possible connections with the appeal of the prophet. First, then, we have to remark that vs.13 constitutes an important element in the portrayal of the woman. With its twofold enclosing *bānayik* [1]) the verse clearly describes the supposed Zion as

---

[1]) The text-critical evidence for 'your sons' (*bānayik* : MT, LXX) has been impaired by 1QIs[a], which reads 'your builders' (*bwnyky* : cf. BHK[3] and BHS). The same applies to Isa. xlix 17, where also other versions support the variant (cf. ibd.).—We are inclined to regard as wrong that interpretation which wants to substitute 'your builders' for 'your sons'. The latter continues the topic of vss. 1 ff., the former is not required by the

mother rather than in terms of the more common daughter-symbol. This leads to a double effect. First the identity of the addressed city with the mother-figure at the beginning of the chapter is stressed. The woman who was summoned there to enlarge the space of her tent for her children is the same as the mother who receives here the assurance that her children will live in great peace within the newly erected walls. So, within its context vs.13 should be understood in such a way that also those who return from far belong to her children, who will be taught by Yhwh and enjoy an abundance of peace. This is entirely in keeping with a passage that we quoted before because of its striking affinity to ours : Isa. xlix 14-26 (cf. especially vss.17 f. 20 ff. 25).

Secondly, we can perhaps also find an allusion to the wife-figure in the line : "Behold, I will set your stones in antimony" (11). All the commentaries mention that this dark mineral powder was used as an eye-pigment and they refer to Jezebel (2 Ki. ix 30) and to the adulterous daughter of Zion (Jer. iv 30). North has commented on this verse as follows : "In this verse the profile of Zion, Yahweh's bride, 'made-up' with eye-paint, shines through the picture of her as a city (cf.Rev.xxi.2). Such a figure is so daring, even in an architectural context, that attempts have been made to disguise (AV, RV, 'fair colours') or to emend the text" [1]). By this remark North continues the interpretation that stems from Jerome : "In stibio, in similitudinem comptae mulieris quae oculos pingit stibio ut pulchritudinem significet civitatis" [2]).

Finally the two characteristics of the new city, its splendid beauty and the divine guarantee for security, constitute the reversal of the woman's distress as described in the first part of the chapter : instead of shame and confusion (4) radiant brilliance attends her (11b-12), instead of fear (4) firm security will be her ground (14-17).

Not less essential are the ties that connect vss.11-17 to vss.7-10. The comparison with Noah, as we have seen, has placed Israel's new epoch of everlasting grace within the context of creation. As the exis-

---

context since it is Yhwh himself who builds the city (cf. North, o.c., p. 251). J. Barr has explained the text-critical situation most satisfactoriously by pointing out that here we meet a *'al-tiqrê*, a kind of rabbinic interpretation which while departing from the Massoretic text strives for the production of multiple meanings : "The interpreter may know perfectly well the general usage and reference of a word at the same time as he is producing an artificial analysis of it in quite another sense" (*Comparative Philology and the Text of the Old Testament*, Oxford 1968, pp. 45 f.).

1) North, o.c., p. 252.

2) PL 24,521.

tence of the earth will never again be jeopardized by the flood, so will God's anger never again threaten the survival of the woman Israel (9). The covenant of God's peace is a firmer ground to live upon than the mountains and the hills (10). Now the new city to be built by God comes up to the expectations that were nourished by the Noah comparison. Only a city the foundations of which God has laid (11b) can claim a stability that equates the firmness of the mountains. Its beauty and the richness of the materials used are not paid for by exposure to foreign arms (15 ff.) and that because the smith who produces the weapon has been created by the same God (16) who is now founding this city. The parallel lines *hinnēh 'ānōkî marbîṣ* (11b) and *hinnē 'ānōkî bārā'tî* (16) extol the city to a future of security that lies beyond the realm of history. Only a builder who is Creator at the same time can make good the oath of vs.10.

Several words come to strenghten the creation background of this founding act. First of all the world that runs parallel to *marbîṣ*, i.e. *wîsadtîk* : "I shall lay your foundations with sapphires" (11). DI uses the root *ysd* for God's founding the earth and parallel to his stretching out the heavens (xlviii 13; li 13.16; cf. xl 21). In xliv 28 *ysd* refers to Cyrus' decision to re-establish the temple in a context that draws a parallel between this fulfilment of God's purpose and his command to the deep to dry up. It is evident that *ysd* in liv 11 strenghtens the suggestion that the founding of this city is a truly creative act.—A second word with the same impact is *tikkônānî* (14) [1]). In xlv 18 *kûn* refers to the creation of the earth while combining the meaning aspects of *ysr* and *'śh*. Elsewhere, it has an ironic connotation : man tries to set up an image that will not move (xl 20) and the oppressor sets himself to destroy (li 13), but this search for firmness is doomed to failure before Yhwh the Creator (xl 18; li 13).

Finally most important in this series is the word *ṣedāqâ*, which encloses the blessing-section of God's personal address (14-17). At its first occurrence (14) it runs parallel to *šālôm* and in this way it is connected to 'the covenant of my peace' (10), the climax of the previous section and the embodiment of God's oath. At the end of the passage *naḥălâ* is the parallel word. The section which is enclosed by *ṣedāqâ* gives evidence of what authors have generally acknowledged as its field of meaning in DI. *ṣedāqâ* is the state of peace, well-being and

---

1) The form is generally considered as a hitpo'lel with assimilation of the second *taw*.

prosperity that derives from God's saving intervention (*ṣedeq*) on behalf of Israel. Yet, as creation and salvation are linked up in DI, so *ṣ^e^dāqâ* assumes cosmic dimensions. That Israel has no reason to be afraid of anyone at all is finally due to the might of the Creator over anyone who produces weapons and wants to stir up strife with Israel (16 f.). *ṣ^e^dāqâ* not only expresses the state of peace which ensues from God's specific relation to this city, it is part of the new world order, which God is going to introduce by his creative and salvific word [1]). Suffice it to quote the following text : "Shower, o heavens, from above and let the skies rain down righteousness (*ṣedeq*) ; let the earth open, that salvation may sprout forth, and let it cause righteousness (*ṣ^e^dāqâ*) to spring up also ; I the Lord have created it" (xlv 8 ; cf. li 6 ff.).

However much it is true that in DI's view *ṣ^e^dāqâ* originates from God's creative power, at the same *ṣ^e^dāqâ* belongs to this people, it will be their *ṣ^e^dāqâ*. The fact that the term assumes a suffix which refers not to God (xlvi 13 ; li 6.8) but to Israel shows to what extent this city will be the concentration of God's creative activity. At the end of his prophecies, in his vision of the new era, the prophet is able to proclaim God's *ṣ^e^dāqâ* as Israel's possession. God's desire for Israel's *šālôm* and *ṣ^e^dāqâ*, which had looked to be so far away (xlviii 18 [2]) ; cf. xlvi 12 f.), is about to find fulfilment. This world order, which originates in God so much so that it is paramount to his word and his strength (xlv 23 f.), will be from now on 'the heritage of his servants'. It will be theirs as much as the desolate land (xlix 8) [3]). The place where Israel will dwell in God's everlasting love, is not a fortuitous choice of history, it belongs to the new order of the world under the covenant.

The last phenomenon that deserves mention is the change from the 2d. person singular to the 3d. person plural in the last stichos of the chapter. God still addresses the woman who represents the city (17a), but the *ṣ^e^dāqâ* which he announces is called 'the heritage of his servants'. Again the children (13) of the woman enter on the scene : those

---

[1]) Cf. K. HJ. FAHLGREN, *ṣ^e^dāḳā, nahestehende und entgegengesetzte Begriffe im Alten Testament*, Uppsala 1932, pp. 97-106 ; H. H. SCHMID, *Gerechtigkeit als Weltordnung* (Beiträge zur hist. Theol. 40), Tübingen 1968, pp. 130-134 ; J. J. SCULLION, "*Ṣedeq-ṣedaqah* in Is. 40-66", *Ugarit-Forschungen* 3 (1971), pp. 335-348.

[2]) This is the only other instance in DI where *ṣ^e^dāqâ* has a suffix referring to Israel. —The suffixes of *ṣedeq* refer only to God : xli 10 ; xlii 21 ; li 5.

[3]) There is one other instance for *naḥălâ* : "I was angry with my people, I profaned my heritage" (xlvii 6).

who are taught by Yhwh are the people that will live in this city as his servants [1]). What they will be taught can be inferred from elsewhere. Yhwh teaches Israel the way she should go, the way that embraces both his commandments and the flight out of exile, the way that results in her *šālôm* and *ṣᵉdāqâ* (xlviii 17-22) [2]). In this manner her children will become God's servants. Up to the very end the woman of the chapter can only be seen as mother. It is this aspect of her multiple identity which warrants the future. For all the stress on the presentic character of God's intervention (11b : "Behold, I am setting your stones") the sight of the future is not lost. The woman who represents the city, will be the mother of God's servants.

* * *

Recapitulating this second part of our inquiry we may say : the woman spoken to in Ch. liv is throughout the same person. She appears under the three shapes that symbolize the three epochs of her existence : mother, wife and city. The prophet addresses her as mother (1-3) and wife (4-6). God has first himself introduced by means of the prophet's message as her lover, who will never depart (7-10). Then he personally addresses the woman in her actual state, i.e. as representing both the miserable city and the oppressed exiles who long for return. He announces that he is going to rebuild her, endowing her with unprecedented beauty and security (11-17).

III. The conception of corporate personality in Isa. liv

We have now ascertained the unity of the chapter from both the structural and thematic angle. The unity is embodied by one single woman : she is throughout the chapter the one person addressed, first by the prophet, then by God himself. Mother, wife and city : the one Israel of different phases of history, manifold in her manifestations, one and unique because of God's election. This multiple identity cannot be understood except in terms of corporate personality. At the end of

---

1) Muilenburg, o.c., p. 641.

2) *lmd* occurs with a more specific object in xl 14 (*'ōraḥ mišpāṭ*, i.e. the course of history : cf. my article mentioned on p. 29, note 3, pp. 9 ff.) and in l 4 with regard to the Servant (*lāda'at lā'ût 'et-yā'ēp*).

this inquiry it is worth projecting our results against the background of that conception as it has been described by H. W. ROBINSON.

He mentions as the first aspect of this phenomenon "the unity of its extension both into the past and into the future" [1]). In Isa. liv Israel is extended into the past in such a way that she includes her ancestress. Or even better, in the present destiny of Israel that of Sarah is repeated, so much so that it is hard to find a clear-cut distinction between them. The appellatives 'barren one, who did not bear... you who have not been in travail' (1a) apply more to the ancient matriarch than to the personification of the actual Israel (if the term personification suits the conception of corporate personality). On the other hand, the statement of vs.1b shows that the prophet is not addressing the wife of Abraham, but the actual Israel because Sarah was not barren in opposition to married women (*mibbᵉnê bᵉʿûlâ*), but although married (Gen. xx 3 : *wᵉhiwʾ bᵉʿulat bāʿal*) she had no children. Moreover, the word *šômēmâ* evokes the national lament of the exilic time.

The summons to joy (1) and the call to enlarge the tent-space (2) apply equally to the ancestress and her progeny. The first half of vs.3 can likewise be understood of both figures, but the end of the verse (3bβ) refers to the present situation while the middle line (3bα), being a combination of formulae that occur in Genesis and Deuteronomy, makes the ancestress and her progeny merge into each other. We conclude that a real distinction is impossible. The person addressed is both Sarah and the people to whom the prophet has been sent by God.

With regard to the woman's second manifestation it is harder to speak of an extension into a figure of the past, because the forsaken woman is not an individual person of remote ages that can be pointed to. Nevertheless, this much is clear : the prophet describes the coming consolation in imagery which has become a major symbol of Israel. In the preaching of the pre-exilic prophets, she is the chosen, yet unfaithful wife of Yhwh. Thus, if there is no extension of the present people into a historical person, there is at least an extension of the present group into the symbolic representation of their forbears so that their identity through the ages is presupposed. The woman who has been married and abandoned is going to be called back by her husband. We have seen that we ought to understand the terms *bōʿălayik* and *gōʾălēk* (5) in a metaphorical sense : Israel's husband is neither a new one nor

[1]) Cf. the article quoted on p. 29, note 1, pp. 50 f.

akin to her former one, but her first one. Thus, *bō'ălayik*, *gō'ălēk* and *qerā'āk* form a climax, each succeeding term correcting the preceding one. "He calls you (back)" in parallelism with "The wife of one's youth, will she be rejected?" constitutes the most appropriate element of the wife-husband symbolism and embodies the extension of the present Israel into the past.

The third symbol, the city, constitutes the present manifestation of Israel. The town in ruins, void of beauty and security, is the most actual representation of the people since the inhabitants of the land as well as the group in exile long for its restoration. It is precisely the identification of city with mother and wife which brings about the corporate personality and makes it the one underlying basis of the chapter. At the same time the city symbol establishes a bridge from the present to the future. The fact that Yhwh himself reconstructs it out of materials that far exceed the conditions of the present age, furnishes it with traits which make it seem to belong to a distant, golden future. This city is destined to be built upon the new world order (*ṣedāqâ*) that comes from God. The well-being (*šālôm*) that God announces is not one of the immediate future : it reaches at least as far into the future as it does into the past.

As a second characteristic of the conception of corporate personality Robinson mentions its realism, "which distinguishes it from 'personification' and makes the group a real entity actualized in its members" [1]). Applied to our chapter this means that Israel is not depicted as Sarah; we should rather say : in Israel's present switch from loneliness to being surrounded by a large brood Sarah herself exchanges the lament for jubilation, just as "Rachel weeps because she dies in her children" (Jer. xxxi 15) [2]). The absence of the names Israel (or Jerusalem) and Sarah bears witness to this fact that, after all, one entity is envisaged. The same holds true for the third symbol, the city. The name of Jerusalem does not occur with the following beneficial effects. First of all, the real identity of the pre-exilic Israel (wife) with the present people who consider Jerusalem as the center of their very existence (city) is suggested. Secondly, both the people in the homeland and those in exile may feel addressed since the building oracle does not address a topographically determined conglomerate of stones but a person representing a collective. Her appellatives apply to all those

---

1) Ibd., pp. 50,51 ff.

2) Ibd., p. 53.

who consider themselves children of that city wherever they may live. The identity of wife and city is not an absurd literary invention but springs from the reality of a people which has once been rooted on the same ground, then dispersed and will now gather in one city which cannot be compared with the present Jerusalem in beauty, security and stability.—The realistic character of the second symbol is harder to describe because, as we have seen, there is no such forsaken woman, an individual of past times who represents the people and lived through its destiny. The realism of the image lies in this that it stands for a clearly defined period of Israel's existence, i.e. for the real, historical sojourn in the country. The prophets, from Hosea on, had introduced this image and availed themselves of it to the extent of making it stand for that particular epoch. So, the totality of the present Israel is addressed under the manifestation of the pre-exilic Israel, symbolized by the wife who longs for her husband. Here the nation is not actualized in one of its individual members, but in the symbol of one of its particular, historical forms of existence.

A third aspect of the Hebrew conception of corporate personality in ROBINSON's view is "the fluidity of reference, facilitating rapid and unmarked transitions from the one to the many, and from the many to the one" [1]. In Isa. liv we are faced with a people that goes its way through history. The fluidity of reference regards the three personifications which stand for distinct periods of Israel's existence. More particularly, in vs.1b the symbols of the desolate mother and the married wife together provide a comparison which announces a new future of fertility. In vss.4-6 the variety of female symbols applied to Israel (nubile girl, widow, forsaken woman, wife of youth) involves that the whole period of her life under the covenant is covered : from Egypt to the desolation of the exile. In vss.11-17 the reference is from the city back to the ancestress by means of the promise of peace for her children and to the wife by means of the description of her radiant beauty.—In short, the actual, still chosen people is addressed throughout the chapter under the three manifestations that are characteristic of the three successive stages of its existence. The fluidity of reference from one manifestation to the other strengthens the one identity of the woman who is spoken to.

So far we have been using the terms 'symbol', 'image' and 'manifes-

---

[1]) Ibd., pp. 50,53 f.

tation'. It is not redundant to examine the customary stylistic categories as for their applicability to the Hebrew conception of corporate personality [1]). Of the three tropes which authors traditionally distinguish, i.e. synecdoche, metonymy and metaphor, we can pass over the first one for it is clear that ancestress, wife and city fall within the definition of a subdivision of synecdoche : a figure of speech by which a part is put for the whole. In our case, however, the quantitative relation [2]) between image and what it represents is of less interest. The two other tropes partly apply to the images used in Ch. liv and partly contain a trait that does not hold true.

Metonymy is usually defined as "a figure of speech which consists in substituting for the name of a thing the name of an attribute of it or of something closely related" [3]). In other words, the relation is of qualitative nature : image and what it represents belong to the same sphere of space, time or conception [4]). According to this current understanding we may characterize the images of ancestress, wife and city as metonymy as far as this qualitative relation is concerned. The image of ancestress falls within the category of cause instead of effect, the city represents the people who live in it (space instead of content) and the wife stands for Israel as she has been portrayed by the prophets (ideal instead of ethnic appearance).—So far the definition of metonymy applies. It does not apply in that it contains an element of substitution : "the name of one thing is used for that of another". The underlying view is that of two separate entities which exchange their names because of their reciprocal relation. The Hebrew conception of corporate personality, on the contrary, tends more to envisage one entity under various manifestations. It would be far too little to say : Israel is addressed as if she were her ancestress, or : instead of the inhabitants the city receives the promise of its restoration. Any idea of separate things which are linked up by ties of space, time or causality and share their names, is alien to the Hebrew conception of world and history. For this reason, the category of metonymy is out of tune with the anthropological presuppositions of corporate personality.

---

1) Our explanation is based on the following works : G. GERBER, *Die Sprache als Kunst*, 2 vols., Berlin 1885²; E. KÖNIG, *Stilistik, Rhetorik, Poetik in Bezug auf die biblische Literatur*, Leipzig 1900; C. F. P. STUTTERHEIM, *Het begrip metaphoor*, Amsterdam 1941; W. KAYSER, *Das sprachliche Kunstwerk*, Bern 1971¹⁵.

2) Cf. KÖNIG, o.c., p. 50.

3) *The Oxford English Dictionary*, Oxford 1961², vol. VI, p. 398.

4) Cf. GERBER, o.c. II, pp. 55-66.

Likewise, the term metaphor only partly serves for the literary expression of corporate personality. Modern linguistic research has emphasized that this particular figure of speech is neither based on the substitution of one word for another nor on the comparison of one thing with another on grounds of some kind of resemblance. A metaphor, in the present view, is rather a trope in which "two thoughts of different things are active together and supported by a single word, or phrase whose meaning is a resultant of their interaction" [1]). In other words, a metaphor ensues from the literary interaction of a principal and a subsidiary subject in such a way that a system of associations characteristic of the latter is applied to the former. It needs no explanation that, as far as this interaction is concerned, the category of metaphor suits fairly well the devices of imagery which are the literary expression of the conception of corporate personality. The total design of our chapter is not badly rendered if we understand the historical manifestations of ancestress, wife and city as interacting as subsidiary addressees with the principal person addressed, the chosen people. "The metaphor selects, emphasizes, suppresses, and organizes features of the principal subject by implying statements about it that normally apply to the subsidiary subject" [2]). In this process, the absence of names and the inadequacy of the epithets that are used for the woman (as well as for God) play their role. On the other hand, the category of metaphor in Western literature, ever since Aristotle, presupposes a profound difference between the spheres to which the two interacting subjects belong. This element of the definition is embodied in the expression *κατὰ τό ἀνάλογον* [3]), which returns, in some form or other, in all the

---

[1]) I. A. Richards, *The Philosophy of Rhetoric*, Oxford 1936, p. 93. This interpretation of the metaphor as an interaction has been elaborated by M. Black, *Models and Metaphors. Studies in Language and Philosophy*, Ithaca N.Y. 1966[3], pp. 25-47.—It may be asked whether this definition of metaphor is really new. König (o.c., p. 93) defines it much in the same way : "Die Metapher entspringt aus der Zusammenschau vergleichbarer Momente des sinnlich wahrnehmbaren und des ideellen Gebietes...". In my view, 'Zusammenschau' is the reverse side of 'interaction'.

[2]) Black, o.c., p. 45.

[3]) Aristotle gives a larger definition of metaphor in *Poetica*, ch. 21 : "Metaphor is the application to one thing of a name belonging to another thing; the transference may be from the genus to the species, from the species to the genus, or from one species to another, or it may be a matter of analogy". The first and second subdivisions cover our category of synecdoche, the third is generally understood to cover what we call metonymy (see however Stutterheim, o.c., p. 75) and the fourth is our metaphor strictly speaking. The last one is subsequently defined by Aristotle as follows :" I

better [1]) definitions of metaphor from the history of literary criticism. The very requirement of some kind of resemblance indicates that the objects compared in terms of their relation to their own sphere belong to basicly divergent areas of being. The same understanding comes to light in the quite common opinion that metaphor springs from fancy while synecdoche is a product of observation and metonymy one of reasoning [2]). Be this as it may, Western literary criticism has always stressed the fact that the metaphor and what it stands for represent essentially divergent spheres of reality [3]). It is precisely this part of the traditional definition which does not fittingly describe the background of corporate personality. The understanding of world and man which underlies this conception is one of unity, of fluid confines between different ontological spheres, in our case between individuals and their community, between succeding epochs and the continuity of national identity, between groups of the population that have come to live in different countries with all the resulting human variety and their fundamental oneness in God's election.—Thus, the classical category of metaphor, like that of metonymy, falls short of what the conception of corporate personality wishes to express [4]). Mainly by way of contrast they illustrate Israel's outlook upon life.

---

explain metaphor by analogy as what may happen when of four things the second stands in the same relationship to the first as the fourth to the third; for then one may speak of the fourth instead of the second, and the second instead of the fourth. And sometimes people will add to the metaphor a qualification appropriate to the term which has been replaced" (ibd.; translation of T. S. DORSCH in : *Classical Literary Criticism* [Penguin Classics], Harmondsworth 1967[2], p. 61). For the further interpretation of this figure of speech in the course of history, cf. GERBER, o.c. II, pp. 19-31, 72-113.

[1]) Misinterpretation of the true nature of the metaphor has not been wanting : cf. GERBER, o.c. II, pp. 27 ff., 74-90 and STUTTERHEIM, o.c., passim.

[2]) GERBER, o.c. II, pp. 23, 49, 76.

[3]) Cf. KÖNIG's definition (quoted on p. 68, note 1) and his subdivisions : transference from the inanimate to the inanimate, from the inanimate to the living, from the living to the living, from the living to the inanimate (o.c., pp. 95-105).

[4]) An exception must be made for the romantic use of metaphor. KAYSER has touched upon this phenomenon in the following remark : "Während bei den Barockdichtern durch den Verstand zwei selbständige Elemente zu einer Mischung—im streng physikalischen Sinne des Wortes—verbunden wurden, entstand in den letzten (viz. romantic) Beispielen in dem Glutstrom des Empfindens oder der Visionen eine Verbindung, die die Autonomie der Elemente aufhebt und aus ihnen ein Neues, Drittes macht" (o.c., p. 124). Especially where he describes the romantic outlook upon reality, his portrayal could stand for the Hebrew conception of world, which underlies the corporate personality : "Ihnen war alles Seiende geheimnisvoll verbunden, so dass es keine festen Grenzen zwischen den Dingen gab, und alles war in stetem Fluss und steter Verwandlung" (o.c., p. 125).

***

Recapitulating our inquiry against the background of this third paragraph we may say : the Hebrew conception of corporate personality constitutes the anthropological mould in which Isa. liv has been cast. It is precisely this view upon man and history that accounts for the multiple identity of the one woman addressed. Her three manifestations of ancestress, wife and city in their interrelationship, such strange composition from the literary point of view, simply embody the three major phases of the history of this one people Israel. Nevertheless, anthropology is not the last ground of her unity. The identity of the ancestress (1-3) and the wife (4-6) on the one hand with the city (11-17) on the other hand can be explained by the course of history. However, it receives a deeper foundation in God's promise that he will love her with everlasting fidelity (7-10). Only in this way is Israel's last manifestation not a city in ruins but one made of precious stones, founded on God's new world order. The one people Israel is God's chosen people.*

*) I am greatly indebted to my friends H. Leene (Amsterdam, Free University) and J. Powers (Berkeley, Graduate Theological Union), the former for discussing the present subject with me, the latter for correcting the English of this article.

KINGSHIP IN THE BOOK OF HOSEA

BY

A. GELSTON

Durham

"They have set up kings, but not by me; they have made princes, and I knew it not". (viii 4)

"Where now is thy king, that he may save thee in all thy cities? and thy judges, of whom thou saidst, Give me a king and princes? I have given thee a king in mine anger, and have taken him in my wrath".

(xiii 10,11).

There can be no doubt that Hosea's attitude to the monarchy of Israel was hostile. But there are at least three ways in which his indictment may be understood. It may refer simply to the actual dissolution of the northern monarchy under a succession of revolutions in Hosea's own time. It may be a far more radical opposition in principle to any form of human kingship over the people of God. Or Hosea's stance may be based on a belief in the 'divine right' of the Davidic dynasty of Judah, coupled with a dismissal of the separate northern monarchy as apostate. The purpose of this paper is briefly to review some of the evidence in the Book of Hosea in an attempt to determine the true basis of the prophet's opposition to the monarchy.

The question is complicated by the perennial problem of sifting the genuine utterances of Hosea from later strands of material which have become absorbed into the corpus of tradition which now constitutes the Book of Hosea. To this must be added many uncertainties of text and interpretation, which are perhaps in any case too considerable to allow a definitive answer to our question [1]).

Before we begin the discussion at all, we must consider briefly the

---

[1]) For a recent general review cf. F. Langlamet, "Les récits de l'institution de la royeauté (I Sam. VII-XII)", *Revue Biblique* 77 (1970), pp. 161-200. For a review of older work on Hosea cf. J. de Fraine, *L'Aspect Religieux de la Royeauté Israélite*, (Analecta Biblica 3), Rome 1954, especially pp. 147-153. References to Wolff and Rudolph in the following discussion denote their respective commentaries (BK XIV 1^2, 1965 and KAT XIII 1, 1966). Biblical quotations in English are from the Revised Version. The following editions of the text and versions have been used : Biblia Hebraica Stutt-

thoery of NYBERG [1]). His starting-point is the obscure king Jareb of v 13 [2]). Since the people resort to him for healing, which in vi 1 and xi 3 is a function of Yahweh, NYBERG infers that he is not in fact a human king at all but a deity called Melek. He goes on to argue that the word מלך in Hosea generally denotes this deity rather than an earthly king. He anticipates the objection that the Old Testament was familiar with a deity Molech, and that מלך would surely have been vocalized in this way in Hosea had it referred to a deity, with the argument that by the time the pronunciation was fixed by the Massoretes no recollection had survived of such a deity in the northern kingdom. A few pages later [3]) NYBERG interprets the king and princes of vii 3 as a reference to this same deity Melek and his heavenly courtiers, the שרים being mythical attendants of the deity. We are not surprised then to find that he interprets viii 4 in terms of the Israelites making themselves deities besides Yahweh, while the king and princes of xiii 10 are also identified as the god Melek and his mythical courtiers.

This interpretation has not commended itself to recent commentators, though H. CAZELLES [4]) argues that NYBERG's hypothesis makes better sense of viii 4 in the overall context, which is concerned with religious apostasy rather than political affairs. He adds the argument that ממשא in viii 10—"they begin to be minished by reason of the burden of the king of princes"—may be interpreted in the same sense as the verb נשא in Amos v 26—"ye have borne Siccuth your king and Chiun your images"—viz. of the carrying of the images of gods in processions. He thinks this interpretation of מלך is appropriate also in iii 4 and v 14 (*sic*), but is cautious about extending it to other passages. In particular he takes the reference in xiii 10 f. to be to a human king. NYBERG's argument is also accepted by G. ÖSTBORN [5]), who regards מלך as a title of Baal.

gartensia, 1970, ed. K. ELLIGER; Septuaginta, ed. A. RAHLFS, 5th edition, Stuttgart 1952; The Bible in Aramaic, ed. A. SPERBER, Leiden 1962; Translatio Syra Pescitto Veteris Testamenti ex codice Ambrosiano Sec. Fere VI photolithographice edita, ed. A. M. CERIANI, Milan 1876-1883; Biblia Sacra iuxta vulgatam versionem, ed. R. WEBER. Stuttgart 1969.

1) H. S. NYBERG, *Studien zum Hoseabuche* (Uppsala Universitets Årsskrift 1935: 6),

2) *op. cit.*, p. 39.

3) *ib.*, pp. 46f.

4) "The Problem of the Kings in Osee viii. 4", *Catholic Biblical Quarterly* xi (1949), pp. 14-25.

5) *Yahweh and Baal*, Studies in the Book of Hosea and related documents (Lunds Universitets Årsskrift, N.F. Avd.1, Bd.51, Nr.6, 1955). See especially pp. 23, 34, 38, 54-57.

It would of course be difficult to disprove NYBERG's hypothesis absolutely. But we do in fact possess a certain knowledge of Canaanite religion, in which Hosea's Baal is amply attested, whereas EISSFELDT could roundly declare that there never was a god called Melek [1])! There is also the indisputable fact that the name Molech, so vocalized in distinction from the ordinary מֶלֶךְ, was familiar to the Old Testament tradition from the seventh century, and Rudolph points out [2]) that a comparison of Jeremiah xix 5—"and have built the high places of Baal, to burn their sons in the fire for burnt offerings unto Baal"— and xxxii 35—"And they built the high places of Baal... to cause their sons and their daughters to pass through the fire unto Molech"—shows that Molech was identified with Baal in Judah. It is hard to imagine how such an interpretation of מלך in Hosea was lost completely, not only in Massoretic times, but even at the period when the oldest versions were made. For there is no evidence in any of them that מלך in Hosea ever has any other than its normal designation: 'king'. RUDOLPH further points out [3]) that NYBERG's argument from healing in v 13 presses the metaphor beyond legitimate limits, and [4]) in relation to the argument that the context in viii 4 is concerned with idolatry rather than with king-making he remarks that since the time of Jeroboam I the two had been closely connected, and that the connection of thought in viii 4 is that both king-making and idol-making were merely human activities. One might note further the allusions to alliances in vv. 8-10 and to military fortifications in v. 14; in fact ch. viii is a collection of oracles protesting against Israel putting her trust in various alternatives to Yahweh, some of which are religious and some political. The final argument against NYBERG's hypothesis is the intrinsic probability of an exegesis of the relevant passages in which the word מלך is understood in its usual sense as denoting a human king; this argument is cumulative.

The concordance reveals some sixteen occurrences of מלך in Hosea outside the two passages with which we are primarily concerned. We may dispose of six of these at once. The title verse (i 1), in which the word occurs twice, is of significance only for the editorial dating of Hosea, while v. 1 simply addresses the royal house alongside the priests

---

1) Cited by J. BEGRICH, *Orientalistische Literaturzeitung* 42 (1939), col. 481.

2) p. 197.

3) p. 125.

4) p. 163.

and the 'house of Israel'. The mysterious king Jareb of v 13 and x 6 is most probably to be explained as the 'Great King', i.e. the King of Assyria [1]), but in any case he is clearly some non-Israelite king. Similarly the reference in xi 5 is explicitly to the Assyrian king.

To these six instances of מלך we should probably add that in viii 10—"they begin to be minished by reason of the burden of the king of princes". We have already noted the general improbability of CAZELLES' interpretation in terms of processions of images of the gods. We cannot afford to overlook the interesting reading of the LXX— *καὶ κοπάσουσιν μικρὸν τοῦ χρίειν βασιλέα καὶ ἄρχοντας* ("and they shall cease for a little anointing a king and princes"), presupposing וְיֶחְדְּלוּ for וַיָּחֵלּוּ, מִמְּשַׁח for מִמַּשָּׂא, and וְ before שָׂרִים. If genuine, this reading would suggest a criticism of the series of revolutions in the Israelite monarchy, such as we find elsewhere in the book, but the objection that nothing is known of any anointing of princes seems decisive. The most likely exegesis of this passage is that of WOLFF, who refers it to the Assyrian king and compares the title šar šarrâni. He takes משא to denote tribute as in II Chronicles xvii 11, and interprets the passage as depicting the divine punishment of Israel for making defensive alliances with the great powers in the form of an impossible burden of tribute imposed by those powers, under which Israel will writhe [2]). This exegesis is followed by RUDOLPH, who also compares the thought of Isaiah x 8, where the Assyrian asks : "Are not my princes all of them kings?" If this interpretation is right, this passage affords no evidence for the elucidation of Hosea's indictment of the Israelite monarchy.

We turn now to the three passages in which the remaining nine instances of מלך occur. We may begin with vii 3-7. In v.3 the king and princes are made glad by the wickedness and deceitfulness of the people —"They make the king glad with their wickedness, and the princes with their lies." The emendation of יְשַׂמְּחוּ to יִמְשְׁחוּ is not only without basis in text or versions; it is also open to the same objection as the LXX reading in viii 10, viz. that nothing is known of the anointing of princes. V.5 refers to the "day of our king", which should probably be emended to read as in the Targum "the day of their king" in view of the context. Whether this is the day of the king's accession, or its

---

1) So WOLFF, RUDOLPH.
2) Revocalizing וַיָּחֵלּוּ as וְיָחִילוּ.

anniversary, or the day of his assassination, is in no way indicated. In v.7 we read : "They... devour their judges; all their kings are fallen : there is none among them that calleth unto me". The rest of this obscure passage depicts the background of drunken debauchery and intrigue under the imagery of a baker's oven. There are indeed so many obscurities in the details of the text and interpretation of this passage, that it can hardly be used as the basis of any theory. However the statement in v.7 that "all their kings are fallen" is most naturally seen as a reference to the rapid succession of kings in Israel after the death of Jeroboam II, and, as RUDOLPH argues, may be taken as the basis of the interpretation of the passage as a whole. This seems then to be a denunciation of the series of revolutions with which the northern monarchy came to its end, and both WOLFF and RUDOLPH date the passage at the accession of Hoshea, the last of the Israelite kings. If this exegesis is right, the most that can be deduced from this passage is the prophet's denunciation of the series of *coups d'état*, with the suggestion that a people who look for security to such kings as these rather than to Yahweh will be disillusioned. There is nothing here to suggest disapproval of kingship *per se*, but only of the northern monarchy as it had now come to be, and of the principle of succession by revolution.

A similar disillusionment with the actual contemporary monarchy of northern Israel is to be found in the four instances of מלך in ch. x. Those in v.3—"Surely now shall they say, We have no king : for we fear not the LORD; and the king, what can he do for us?"—refer most naturally to Hoshea [1]), and perhaps reflect the period when he was imprisoned by the Assyrians (II Kings xvii 4). The situation is such that the king is unable to do anything for his people; it is as though they no longer had a king. The theme of vv. 7 and 8 seems to be that the king and the cultic centres, the two fundamental institutions of the northern kingdom, will both be destroyed; the king in particular is like flotsam on the water [2]) : "As for Samaria, her king is cut off, as twigs [3]) upon the water. The high places also of Aven, the sin of Israel, shall be destroyed: the thorn and the thistle shall come

---

1) So WOLFF, RUDOLPH.

2) RUDOLPH takes מלך here to be an ironic reference to the calf-image; this of course fits the flotsam metaphor, but the reference of מלך back to the עגלות of v.5 is difficult after the intervening reference to מלך ירב in v.6.

3) So RV margin. See the commentaries *ad loc.*

up on their altars." If נִדְמָה is emended to נִדְּתָה in the light of LXX, Peshiṭta and Vulgate, the further statement is made that Samaria has rejected her king; this however does not seem to correspond to political fact, and would presumably only be a more forcible way of expressing the disillusionment of v.3. V.15 simply states : "at day-break shall the king of Israel be utterly cut off". This is but another expression of the judgement of Yahwah on Israel in the form of cutting off her main support at the critical moment at the outset of battle. None of the references to the king in this chapter then throw any light on the question of Hosea's attitude to kingship in principle; they merely attest the ultimate impotence of the monarchy in face of the disaster threatening Samaria.

The remaining two instances of מלך are in iii 4,5. In v.4 Hosea predicts a lengthy period during which Israel will be deprived of her favourite institutions : "the children of Israel shall abide many days without king, and without prince, and without sacrifice, and without pillar, and without ephod or teraphim." Probably no more than the fact of this deprivation is intended, and the analogy of the preceding verse would suggest that the deprivation will not necessarily be permanent. For the "many days" of v.4 are surely to be interpreted in the light of the "many days" of v.3, and v.3 presumably looks beyond the "many days" of sexual restraint to a closer relationship in the future. The analogy of chapter ii, where a new betrothal lies beyond the coming wilderness experience, supports this interpretation. Presumably both the wilderness experience of chapter ii and the "many days" of iii 4 denote a period of exile, when the national institutions will naturally be in abeyance (cf. ix 3, 15, 17). On the other hand it is likely that Hosea disapproved without qualification of the last three institutions listed in iii 4 : pillar, ephod and teraphim; while a case can be made out for his total rejection of sacrifice (cf. vi 6—"I desire mercy, and not sacrifice; and the knowledge of God more than burnt offerings"), though it is more probable that Hosea repudiated the actual sacrificial cult of his day rather than all sacrifice in principle [1]). It is possible then that in iii 4 Hosea rejects the institution of kings and princes outright, but the verse in itself requires no more than a temporary deprivation of kingship among other Israelite institutions during an impending period of exile.

The following verse is much more interesting and important, but also

---

[1]) Cf. R. de Vaux, *Ancient Israel* (E.T. 1961), pp. 454 f.

much more problematic! Here Hosea anticipates the eventual return of Israel to Yahweh and, as the text stands, to "David their king": "afterward shall the children of Israel return, and seek the LORD their God, and David their king." There is no evidence in text or versions for the omission of this phrase, and it must therefore belong to the early tradition of the book. But it is often regarded as a gloss [1]), in which case it cannot be reckoned as evidence for the standpoint of Hosea himself. If the phrase does derive from Hosea, we have clear evidence that he did not repudiate kingship in principle; at most he will have rejected the northern monarchy as apostate from the Davidic dynasty, itself guaranteed by divine covenant (cf. II Samuel vii). If the phrase is a gloss, the possibility that Hosea rejected kingship in principle remains. The question whether this phrase derives from Hosea himself is therefore crucial for the whole discussion, and must be approached by way of several related questions.

One closely related question is the exegesis and genuineness of another passage: ii 2 (EVV i 11). Here it is said that Israel and Judah are to be reunited and appoint themselves a single head (ראש): "And the children of Judah and the children of Israel shall be gathered together, and they shall appoint themselves one head." This "head" is not further specified, though in conjunction with iii 5 it would be natural to understand it as a reference to the Davidic king, as was already done by the Targumist. It is interesting that the books of Jeremiah (xxx 9, xxxiii 14-26) and Ezekiel (xxxiv 23 f., xxxvii 22 ff.), which both show affinities with the thought of Hosea, should anticipate the reunion of Israel and Judah under the Davidic dynasty, and it is at least possible that the conjunction of Hosea ii 2 and iii 5 in their present form lies behind this expectation in the later books. But even this would only demonstrate that the reference to David in iii 5 was not later than the exilic period; it would not prove that it derived from Hosea himself.

There are however features of ii 2 which are less encouraging to an identification of the "head" with the Davidic king. For one thing it is not easy to envisage what might be meant by the descendants of Judah *appointing* the Davidic king as their head; he was that already both in historical fact and in theological theory. Nor were the Israelites in a position to *appoint* him as king also of Israel. The verbs appro-

---

[1]) So WOLFF, RUDOLPH.

priate to a reunion of Israel and Judah under the Davidic king are the שוב and בקש of iii 5, and not the שים of ii 2. Moreover the choice of the term ראש is odd if the Davidic king is in mind. It is true that Saul is called ראש in I Samuel xv 17, and that the term could therefore denote kingship. But it has a much wider connotation of leadership (cf. Numbers xiv 4, Judges xi 8), and it would be consistent with the view that Hosea repudiated human kingship in principle to argue that the choice of the less specific ראש was in deliberate preference to the concrete מלך. The fact that Hosea never uses מלך as a title of Yahweh is also suggestive in this respect. The language of ii 2 considered in itself suggests a tentative approach : the reunion of Israel and Judah as one political entity and as the people of Yahweh is clearly envisaged, but whether this political entity is to take the form of a monarchy seems to be deliberately left open. If these considerations are well grounded, it seems unlikely that both ii 2 and iii 5 in their present form can derive from Hosea, unless we posit a degree of development in his thought. On the other hand it is easy to see how a Judaean glossator, persuaded independently of the divine right of the Davidic dynasty, could have interpreted ii 2 in terms of a reunion of Israel and Judah under that dynasty, and imported this interpretation into the text of iii 5.

The genuineness of ii 2 itself remains to be considered. It is true that the passage to which it belongs—ii 1-3— follows abruptly on the conclusion of chapter i, and might even be taken to be a contradiction of the prophecy of the symbolic names. But there is further material in chapter ii to substantiate the view that Hosea looked beyond judgment to restoration, and the reversal of the symbolic names is found also in ii 25. The present position of ii 1-3 is no doubt due to the editors, who wanted to introduce a positive note into the prologue of the book [1]). The provenance of the passage as a whole is too complex a question to be treated here, and we must be content with two further observations. One is that if we have to choose between the appointing of one 'head' in ii 2 and "David their king" in iii 5, the specific reference to David is more likely to be a later gloss, as it is consonant with the belief of the exilic age. The more distinctive but less precise expectation of ii 2 is therefore more likely to derive from Hosea. The other observation is that the specific anticipation of a reunion of Israel and Judah is

---

1) So RUDOLPH.

consistent with the prophet's denunciation of aggrandizement on the part of Judah in v 10 [1]). But the whole question of the prophet's attitude to Judah is another of those larger related inquiries which have to be taken into account in the discussion of iii 5. All we can say at this point is that we have found no convincing reasons for denying ii 2 to Hosea, but some grounds for hesitating to think that he was also the originator of the reference to David in iii 5.

Apart from the title verse (i 1) there are fourteen references to Judah in the Book of Hosea. Four of these occur in the passage v 10-14, relating probably to the aggrandizement of Judah during the aftermath of the Syro-Ephraimite war [1]), and reflect an unfavourable attitude to Judah. To these may probably be added vi 4—"O Ephraim, what shall I do unto thee? O Judah, what shall I do unto thee? for your goodness is as a morning cloud, and as the dew that goeth early away." Two others (ii 2 and x 11) place Judah alongside Israel without expressing any estimate of Judah. Two others at the beginning of chapter xii are fraught with difficulty. Verse 1 is notoriously obscure, and may reflect either approval of Judah for her loyalty in contrast to Israel, or disapproval of Judah as equally faithless as Israel! The RV translates (EVV xi 12): "Ephraim compasseth me about with falsehood, and the house of Israel with deceit: but Judah yet ruleth with God, and is faithful with the Holy One." The uncertainty here derives not only from רד, but also from the identification of אל and קדושים and from the relation of v.1 to v.3. The latter verse (EVV xii 2) is also obscure—"The LORD hath also a controversy with Judah, and will punish Jacob according to his ways." As it stands it introduces Yahweh's ריב against Judah, but the passage goes on to indict Jacob. The ו before לפקד has been thought to conceal an originally fuller text, in which case it is likely that as in vi 4 both Israel and Judah are arraigned. In any case the reference to Judah here seems to be unfavourable. The remaining five passages are for various reasons suspect as glosses. Three are parenthetic expansions, applying a judgment against Israel to Judah as well (v 5, vi 11, viii 14), and may well represent a stage in the tradition where Hosea's oracles were reapplied to the southern kingdom, as also seems to have happened with those of Amos. One passage, iv 15—"Though thou, Israel, play the harlot, yet let not Judah offend", seems to reflect a favourable attitude to Judah; but the LXX has a

[1]) Cf. A. Alt, "Hosea v 8—vi 6, Ein Krieg und seine Folgen in prophetischer Beleuchtung" (1919), *Kleine Schriften* II, pp. 163-187.

different text, including *καὶ* before *Ιουδα,* which suggests that here too it is a gloss. Finally, i 7—"But I will have mercy upon the house of Judah..." clearly interrupts the sequence of thought, and seems deliberately inserted to exempt Judah from the judgement of the previous verse. It appears then that we have to allow with WOLFF [1]) and RUDOLPH [2]) for two separate Judaean redactions, one of which exempts Judah from Hosea's strictures against Israel, while the other reapplies them to Judah as well. Neither of the clearly favourable references to Judah can be assigned with any confidence to Hosea, while the favourable interpretation of xii 1 is itself uncertain! It would of course be a dangerous over-simplification to make the attitude to Judah a criterion for the genuineness of a particular passage, but the fact that there is not one certain favourable reference to Judah among the sayings of Hosea weakens the case that Hosea approved of the Davidic dynasty, and that the reference to David in iii 5 is likely to derive from the prophet himself.

The other larger question which has a bearing on the discussion of the reference to David in iii 5 is that of Hosea's historical allusions. There are a number of these and if Hosea regarded the establishment of the separate northern kingdom as an act of apostasy against the divinely appointed Davidic dynasty, it would not be unreasonable to expect among them a clear reference to this event. Most of the historical allusions take the form of a reference to the place at which an event occurred, and most of them are obscure, as may be instanced by the bewildering variety of exegesis of the allusions to the Jacob traditions in chapter xii! The historical references which are relevant for our inquiry are those to Jezreel (i 4), to Gibeah (ix 9, x 9), and to Gilgal (ix 15).

In i 4 the name of the prophet's son Jezreel is the basis of a prophecy that Yahweh will punish the dynasty of Jehu for the massacre of the Omrides at Jezreel; but the judgement will not stop at the extinction of Jehu's dynasty, but will continue until the monarchy (ממלכות) of Israel is brought entirely to end : "I will avenge the blood of Jezreel upon the house of Jehu, and will cause the kingdom of the house of Israel to cease." It is most natural to take this as referring specifically to the northern monarchy, though it would be reading too much into the text to claim that Hosea regarded the revolution of Jehu as the

---

[1]) Pp. xxvif.

[2]) Pp. 25ff.

basic sin which cried out for the total abolition of that monarchy. If, as seems required by the facts of the situation, this prophecy was uttered at latest during the six month reign of Jeroboam II's son Zechariah, and thus early in Hosea's prophetic ministry, it seems that the prophet's initial criticism of the monarchy was inspired by horror at the massacre of the Omrides, but that even at that stage Hosea was conscious of a still more radical evil in the Israelite monarchy which called for its total abolition. There is however no trace here of any criticism of the initial establisment of the separate northern kingdom.

The two references to Gibeah, ix 9 :"They have deeply corrupted themselves, as in the days of Gibeah" and x 9 : "O Israel, thou hast sinned from the days of Gibeah : there they stood; that the battle against the children of iniquity should not overtake them in Gibeah", unfortunately lack any detailed specification of the events the prophet has in mind. The connection of Saul with Gibeah (I Samuel x 26 f., xi) has given rise to the suggestion that Hosea is here alluding to the original institution of the monarchy. But this idea is not very appropriate to the context in either of these passages, and a reference to the events of Judges xix-xxi seems more probable. In any case the actual inauguration of the monarchy was associated not with Gibeah but with Gilgal. The reference to Gilgal in ix 15—"All their wickedness is in Gilgal; for there I hated them"—is unfortunately once again not specific enough to connect it clearly with the inauguration of the monarchy at Gilgal in I Samuel xi 15. In favour of such an interpretation is the mention of the rebelliousness of the princes later in the verse, and the evident importance of the incident in Hosea's mind. Against such an interpretation is the fact that the preceding verses have referred to the first practice of the Baal cult by Israel at Baal-peor (v.10), and that this incident is linked with Gilgal (and Shittim—cf. Numbers xxv 1) in Micah vi 5. In any case it seems more germane to the overall message of Hosea to regard the first practice of the Baal cult as the sum of Israel's wickedness, rather than the institution of the monarchy. If the reference here is to the establishment of the monarchy, it is certainly to its initial establishment under Saul, and not to that of the separate northern monarchy.

At this point it is convenient to sum up our conclusions about the reference to David in iii 5. In the first place it seems not very likely that both it and the prophecy of ii 2 that the reunited Israel and Judah will appoint themselves a single head derive from Hosea himself; of the two, the less specific expectation of ii 2 is much more likely to be original, while the reference to David in iii 5 is easily explained as an interpretation of the earlier passage in the light of the expectation current in the exilic age. The fact that there is not one certain favourable reference to Judah among the sayings of Hosea weakens the hypothesis that the prophet believed in the divine right of the Davidic dynasty, and restricted his criticism of kingship to the separate northern monarchy. It is weakened further by the fact that the only historical allusion which concerns the monarchy is that of i 4 to the massacre of the Omrides by Jehu, while the reference to Gilgal in xi 15, if it is to the monarchy at all, must be to its initial establishment under Saul, though it more probably relates to the cult of Baal-peor. No historical allusion has been found to the setting up of the separate northern kingdom under Jeroboam I. The weight of the evidence then seems to be against the reference to David in iii 5 deriving from the prophet himself, though the possibility cannot be ruled out.

We turn finally to the principal passages with which we are concerned, viii 4 and xiii 10 f. The first of these—"They have set up kings, but not by me; they have made princes, and I knew it not"—accuses Israel of making themselves kings and princes independently of Yahweh, and in itself could refer to the contemporary succession of *coups d'état*, to the establishment of the separate northern monarchy under Jeroboam I, or to the original institution of the monarchy under Saul. The objection to the second possibility, that the separate northern monarchy was originally set up at the instigation of the prophet Ahijah, and would therefore have been approved by Hosea, can hardly be sustained in face of the fact that Hosea clearly repudiated the revolution of Jehu (i 4) despite its having been inspired by the prophetic circle of Elijah and Elisha [1]). One consideration indeed in favour of this second possibility is the fact already noted that the immediate context in viii 4 is that of an indictment of idolatry, coupled with the fact that the Deuteronomist never tires of drawing attention to the great sin of Jeroboam I in introducing the cult of the calf images at Bethel and Dan (I Kings xii 28 f., xv 26, 34, etc.). The further fact that viii 5 goes on to speak of the calf image at first sight encourages us to make such a connection. But in the absence of any specific reference to the establishment of the separate northern monarchy elsewhere in the book, it seems preferable to interpret this verse primarily in relation

---

1) Cf. Rudolph, p. 163.

to the series of dynastic revolutions in the northern kingdom. It is these that have been carried out without regard to Yahweh (cf. i 4 on Jehu). This conclusion is strengthened by a further consideration. There is a difficulty in the text as it stands, in that we should expect הֵשִׂירוּ to be pointed הֵשֵׂרוּ if it is derived from שרר; but in any case nothing is known of any formal appointment of princes such as would be suggested by such an interpretation. Rudolph accordingly accepts the Massoretic interpretation, followed by Rashi and Ibn Ezra, of השירו as a biform of הסירו, which is actually read in some mss., though not supported by any of the versions. This yields the meaning of the RV margin : "They have set up kings, but not by me; they have removed them, and I knew it not." The prophet objects to a theory and practice of kingship in which the king's authority rests on human rather than divine appointment, and may be terminated by human will.

The third possibility, that the prophet refers to the original institution of the Israelite monarchy under Saul, is the most immediately attractive in the case of xiii 10 f., where we can hardly fail to hear the overtones of what is commonly regarded as the source hostile to the establishment of the monarchy in I Samuel viii—xii : "Where now is thy king, that he may save thee in all thy cities? and thy judges, of whom thou saidst, Give me a king and princes? I have given thee a king in mine anger, and have taken him away in my wrath." There may even be a verbal allusion to the people's request in I Samuel viii 6, and it is certainly difficult to see how this could be taken to refer to the establishment of the separate northern monarchy under Jeroboam I. For the rest, this passage merely reinforces the predictions we have noted elsewhere that Israel is to be deprived of her king, and that she will no longer be able to look to him for deliverance. There is indeed a certain inconsistency with viii 4, in that the king is here clearly stated to have been a gift to Israel from Yahweh, albeit a gift made 'in His anger', while the earlier passage speaks of the making and perhaps also of the deposing of kings without reference to Yahweh. This inconsistency may encourage the view that the two passages are making different points, viii 4 being directed against the succession of dynastic revolutions, while xiii 10 f. expresses a fundamental objection to the establishment of a human monarchy in the first place.

But is Hosea so radically opposed to any form of kingship? Most of the references to the kings have proved to relate primarily to the contemporary monarchy in northern Israel. There was some reason to believe that iii 4 may have envisaged a temporary rather than a permanent deprivation of kingship, and the expectation of the reunited Israel and Judah appointing themselves a single head (ii 2) may, despite the apparent preference of ראש to מלך, indicate a cautious optimism on the part of the prophet with regard to the ultimate future of kingship. The allusion in xiii 10 to I Samuel viii 6 is by no means certain, the only words in common being תנה and מלך, and the imperfects in xiii 11 may be taken in an iterative sense [1]: "I keep giving you a king... and taking him away...", in which case the primary reference of this passage too will be to the contemporary monarchy and its revolutions. Even if the king is regarded as gift of Yahweh in response to His people's prayer, this is no guarantee of his permanence. Indeed the very series of revolutions itself is from one point of view the people's sin, from another Yahweh's judgement on their abuse of His gift. One is reminded of the narrative of I Samuel viii in which Samuel is repeatedly told by God to accede to the people's request for a king, although the request itself is seen as a rejection of the kingship of Yahweh. This paradox is sufficient to explain the apparent inconsistency of xiii 10 f. with viii 4. The allusion to the original appointment of Saul, if it is present, will underline the argument that the people's confidence in the institution of kingship, which can be traced right back to its inauguration, is at last to be shown to be misplaced by the king's inability any longer to save his people. This passage then may indicate a fundamental rejection of kingship, but more probably relates once again to the current disillusionment of Israel with the institution of kingship, which Yahweh has now taken away from her.

We have now briefly reviewed the evidence at our disposal, and have reached the conclusion that the prophet's indictment was most probably in each case directed primarily against the actual contemporary monarchy of northern Israel. Hosea saw the monarchy as one of the alternative foci of the people's trust and allegiance, alongside the Baal cult, foreign alliances, etc., and hence as undermining their vestigial loyalty to Yahweh. He was outraged by the nonchalance with which kings were appointed or deposed at will, and by the drunken debauchery or bloody revolution with which this was accompanied. More than once he drew attention to the impotence of the king any longer to

[1] So Wolff, Rudolph. The versions, except the Vulgate (which renders by the future), take as preterites, perhaps reading as Waw consecutives.

save his people, perhaps hoping that in the hour of disillusionment they might yet turn back to their true King—Yahweh!

This does not preclude the possibility of a historical perspective as well, and an allusion to the original establishment of the monarchy under Saul is perhaps probable in xiii 10 and possible though unlikely in ix 15. The hypothesis that Hosea regarded the initial establishment of the monarchy under Saul as wrong in principle is difficult to sustain in relation to viii 4 if we accept the interpretation of השירו as a biform of הסירו. While it is perfectly possible to take xiii 10 f. in this sense, it is not necessary to do so, and it can only be done at the expense of ignoring the cautious optimism that may be detected behind ii 2 and iii 4. It is more likely that Hosea's attitude to kingship, as to sacrifice, was a criticism of the current reality rather than an opposition to the institution in principle.

The theory that Hosea accepted the Davidic dynasty as a divine institution and rejected the separate northern monarchy as apostate can be supported by only two arguments. One is that the reference to David in iii 5 is a genuine utterance of Hosea, in which case its relation to ii 2 needs to be resolved. The other is the connection between king-making and idol-making in viii 4, which, together with the explicit reference to the calf cult in the following verse, might be held to point specifically to Jeroboam I. While this theory must remain a possibility, this evidence is hardly sufficient to sustain it.

The clearer resolution of any one of the many uncertainties confronted in our review of the evidence might lead to a different conclusion. But in the present state of knowledge it is safest to conclude that Hosea's indictment was directed primarily against the northern monarchy of his day, and to refrain from drawing more radical conclusions, whether that he was opposed to kingship in principle, or that he rejected the northern monarchy as apostate from the Davidic dynasty, which he accepted as a divine institution.

THE MASSORETES AS LINGUISTS

BY

J. C. L. GIBSON

Edinburgh

It is not difficult to pick holes in the traditional division of the Tiberian vowels into five 'mothers' and five 'daughters', that is into what we would call five long and five short as in the following table :

	Short			*Long.*	
ַ	[páṯaḥ]	a	ָ	[qǻmɛṣ]	ā
ֶ	[sᵉgól]	e	ֵי ֵ	[ṣeré]	ē ê
ִ	[ḥírɛq]	i	ִי	[ḥírɛq]	î
ֻ	[qibbúṣ]	u	וּ	[šúrɛq]	û
ָ	[qåmɛṣ ḥåṭúp̱]	o	ֹ וֹ	[ḥódlɛm]	ō ô

Thus one sign [qǻmɛṣ] does duty both for the long variety of [páṯaḥ] and the short variety of [ḥólɛm]; one name [ḥírɛq] figures in both columns, and the long and short varieties are distinguished by reference to the presence or absence of 'mothers of the reading' or vowel letters in the biblical orthography; and [qibbúṣ] and [šúrɛq] are called short and long, though the first would seem to be long in a form like שְׁמֻעָה (1 Sam. ii 24) and the second short in a form like כּוּלָם (Jer. xxxi 34). As a matter of fact neither the Tiberian Massoretes in drawing up their system nor such early Jewish grammarians as we have knowledge of take vowel quantity into account, and they distinguish only seven vowels, called 'kings', not ten. It seems to have been the Ḳɪᴍḥɪs in the 12th and 13th centuries who introduced the tenfold arrangement and were in this respect the first 'traditionalists' [1]). In Massoretic times, therefore, [qǻmɛṣ] must have stood for a single sound, normally now transcribed [å] (IPA [ɔ]) [2]) and in quality somewhere be-

[1]) W. Cʜᴏᴍsᴋʏ, *David Ḳimḥi's Hebrew Grammar* (*Mikhlol*) (Philadelphia 1933), § 3a and p. 31, n. 11. The Ḳɪᴍḥɪs were in this as in other matters heavily influenced by the Latin grammar practised in their native Provence.

[2]) IPA = International Phonetic Association

tween [a] and [o], as the form of the sign in some manuscripts (ׇ a combination of [pá̱taḥ] and [ḥólɛm]) implies; not until much later did it come to represent two sounds, when in the Sephardic pronunciation [å] was retained in unstressed closed syllables, but moved to [a] (the same sound as [pá̱taḥ]) elsewhere. The [ḥírɛq] of course denoted a single sound [i], and the presence or otherwise of a vowel letter in the orthography was properly regarded as irrelevant; the Massoretes seem to have realised what it took European scholars many centuries to find out, that the *matres lectionis* had nothing to do with vowel length either, though the dozens of examples in the Bible like the two with [u] vowels just cited should have told them [1]). Finally [qibbúṣ] and [šúrɛq] were alternative signs of the same vowel [u]; in their case the deciding factor in the use of one rather than the other *was* the presence or absence of a vowel letter in the orthography, but since *matres lectionis* were not connected with vowel length, this was a technical graphic matter only. If in spite of all this evidence we still wish to consider vowel quantity more important than the Tiberian Massoretes did, we ought to speak not of long and short vowel signs, but of long and short varieties of all the vowels, depending on the kind of syllable, open, closed, stressed, unstressed, in which they occur [2]); thus, for example,

[qå̆mɛṣ] is long in חָכָם 'wise' and short in חָכְמָה 'wisdom';

but equally

[pá̱taḥ] is long in שָׁמַר 'he kept' and short in מַלְכִּי 'my king';

[sᵉgól] is long in יְגַלֶּה 'he shall reveal' and short in הֶעֱלָה 'he brought up', etc.

This, unlike the traditional division, is a perfectly legitimate view to take, though it is not one that greatly assists the purpose of this paper, since it does not reveal anything about the Massoretes as linguists.

By way of a complete contrast in linguistic method, let us now look at a modern phonemic analysis of the Tiberian vowels, that by S. Morag

---

1) See the lists in A. Sperber, *A Historical Grammar of Biblical Hebrew* (Leiden 1966), pp. 101-2, 564 (§ 2b), 565 (§ 3b). On my own view of the origin of the *matres lectionis* as 'prosodies' see below p. 95 and in more detail *Archivum Linguisticum* 17 (1969), pp. 154ff.

2) So e.g. the excellent scientific *Grammatik* of R. Meyer (Berlin 1966), I, pp. 54ff. The British students' *Grammars* of Weingreen (Oxford 1959), pp. 4 ff., and Davidson-Mauchline (Edinburgh 1962), pp. 13ff., regrettably keep the traditional classification.

in his monograph in the *Janua Linguarum* series [1]). There are others by HARRIS and CANTINEAU [2]), which are different in several details, but his will suffice as a model. MORAG divides the vocalization signs into univalent and bivalent, there being eleven of the former and two of the latter. Nine of the univalent signs represent the seven vowels previously named (/u/ having two signs) plus /ǻ/, [ḥåṭép̱ qå'mɛṣ]. To these eight vowels he assigns phonemic status, in the case of the last as a result of a few oppositions like אֲנִי 'I' and אֳנִי 'ships', or דָּמִי 'my blood' and דֳּמִי 'silence'. The other two univalent signs represent [ă], the [ḥåṭép̱ páṯaḥ] and [ɛ̆], the [ḥåṭép̱ seɡól], which he regards as allophones or non-distinctive variants of /ĕ/ (the [šewå']). The two bivalent signs are the [šewå'] and [dåg̱éš], the first representing both the phoneme /ĕ/ and *zero*, the second the two non-phonemic features of gemination (doubling) and the plosive versus the fricative allophones of the series /pbtdkg/, i.e. what we mnemonically call the *Beghadhkephath* consonants. As regards the full vowels, this analysis accords much more exactly with the actual Tiberian signs than does the traditional division into five short and five corresponding long vowels, and I have adopted a similar for my own transcriptions, i.e. [aɛeiåou]. But in the case of the other signs of the Tiberian system, the [šewå'] and [ḥaṭep̱ím] on the one hand and the [dågéš] point on the other, MORAG's analysis seems to me in its turn to wander far from any conception the vocalizers might have had of their role, and thus it merits from the point of view of this paper the same judgment that has already been passed on the post-ḲIMḤI arrangement of the vowels.

To take the [šewå'] first [3]). According to MORAG the Tiberian Massoretes gave the name [šewå'] to two distinct entities, a murmured vowel sound and *zero* or absence of vowel; but the word [šewå'] means as far as we can tell, 'nothing', so it is surely reasonable to suppose that the Massoretes held the two to be the same. In this respect traditional Jewish grammar in speaking of a 'nothing thatm oves' (שְׁוָא נָד or שְׁוָא נָע) and a 'nothing that stays still' (שְׁוָא נָח) are in fact nearer the

---

1) *The Vocalization Systems of Arabic, Hebrew and Aramaic* ('s Gravenhage 1962), pp. 22-4.

2) Z. S. HARRIS, 'Linguistic Structure of Hebrew', *Journal of the American Oriental Society* 61 (1941), pp. 143 ff., J. CANTINEAU, 'Essai d'une phonologie de l'hébreu biblique', *Bulletin de la Société de Linguistique de Paris* 46 (1950), pp. 107 ff.

3) See further the shrewd study by W. CHOMSKY, 'The Pronunciation of the Shewa', *Jewish Quarterly Review* 62 (1971), pp. 88-94.

truth than MORAG. Similarly, by distinguishing between the full vowels and the [ḥåṭép̱] sounds, traditional grammar follows more closely the Tiberian Massoretes' own thinking; for the fact that these signs are composed of the sign for [š^{e}wå'] plus that for a full vowel is a persuasive argument that they regarded them just as they did the [š^{e}wå' nå'ḏ], as 'nothings' on the move or, to put it another way, as stronger varieties of 'nothing'. If therefore we wish to preserve the Tiberian view of the [š^{e}wå'] and [ḥåṭép̱] signs, we ought to continue in the traditional manner transcribing them by small letters in the upper case [^{eaεå}], that is, see the sounds as operating over or upon a word or phrase, linking together (like *zero*) syllables or syllable parts, rather than as MORAG understands them, discrete sounds of the same kind as the full vowels to be transcribed with them in a linear succession. In this way we will better preserve the syllabic constitution of words and phrases as the Massoretes conceived it. Compare the following written shapes, transcriptions and syllabic structures (C = Consonant; V = vowel) and you will see what I am getting at; the first transcriptions are phonemic of the sort that MORAG would make, the second my own :

דְבַר 'word of' / dĕbar ...'.../; [d^{e}ḇar...'...]; CCVC
יִשְׁאֲלוּ 'they shall ask' / yiš'ĕlú /; [yiš'^{a}lú]; CVC + CCV
דְּבָרְךָ 'your word' / dĕbårĕkå' /; [d^{e}ḇår(^{e})ḵå']; CCV + CCV
יַעֲבֹר 'he will cross' / ya'ĕbór/; [ya(')^{a}ḇór]; CVC + CVC

Two problems immediately confront this view of the [š^{e}wå'] and [ḥåṭép̱] sounds as stronger varieties of 'nothing', yet structurally still 'nothing'. They are highlighted by the bracketed letters in the last couple of transcriptions just offered.

The first is the problem of the so-called *Shewa medium* of traditional grammar, a special category of the [š^{e}wå' nå'ḏ], though there is significantly no equivalent Hebrew term. The problem does not exist for forms like מַלְכֵי 'kings of...', מַלְכוּת 'kingdom', לִנְתּוֹשׁ 'to pluck up', or מְבַקְשִׁים 'seeking', where the first syllable has a traditional short vowel but no [mέṯɛg̱] sign. The [š^{e}wå'] is therefore silent, and these forms should be transcribed [malḵe..'..], [malḵúṯ], [linṯóš], [m^{e}baqším]. That leaves us with forms like חָכְמָה 'she is wise' and חׇכְמָה 'wisdom', where a [š^{e}wå' nå'ḏ] seems to contrast with *zero*, and consequently to be a different phonemic feature. It is interesting that while DAVID ḲIMḤI specifically states that the [š^{e}wå'] in מַלְכֵי is silent, he also specifically states that one following a long vowel is sounded [1]). Is Ḳimḥi wrong here, as on the thesis I have advanced he should be? The only solution I can see is to suggest a rethinking of the function of the [mɛ́tɛg]; it and not a [šᵉwå' nå'd̲] may indicate the phonetic feature, presumably a particular kind of secondary stress, that constitutes the element of contrast with חָכְמָה.

Secondly, there is the problem of the [ḥåṭēp̲] in forms like יַעֲבֹר, which equates in a form without a pharyngal consonant not with [šᵉwå' nå'd̲] but with [šᵉwå' nå'ḥ], e.g. יִשְׁמֹר. Historically speaking I believe that murmured sounds like this [ᵃ] were replacements for pharyngal and laryngal sounds which had lapsed in ordinary speech following the biblical period, and had not yet been restored when the Tiberian system was first invented, a supposition that would at least account for the fricative [b̲] in יַעֲבֹר. Such murmured sounds are regularly indicated in the Greek transliterations of the second column of Origen's Hexapla, e.g. εελιθ for הֶעֱלִיתָ [2]). But it is worth asking further whether the pharyngal or laryngal sounds in these internal positions were ever restored, either in the Massoretic period or subsequently. I find it hard to conceive of a restored consonant and a murmured vowel that had previously occupied its slot both being retained in any natural pronunciation of Hebrew. The resulting syllabic structure would then be CV linked by a connecting vowel to CVC (formerly CVC + CVC). Conversely, in a form like נֶהְפַּךְ 'it was turned' (Ex. vii 15), we have probably to conclude that the laryngal had not previously lapsed, or if it had, that it had been restored before the vocalizers got to work.

Finally on the subject of the [šᵉwå'], I would like briefly to mention the Palestinian supralinear system, which possessed no sign equivalent to the [šᵉwå'], but occasionally wrote the sign of a full vowel where the Tiberian system has a [šᵉwå' nå'd̲], as for example in לעת = לְעֵת

———

1) *David Ḳimḥi's Hebrew Grammar*, §§ 3c, 5c with Chomsky's notes. My statement in *Journal of Linguistics* 2 (1966), Additional Note A, p. 42, should be corrected in the light of the argument here.

2) Further examples in A. Sperber, *op. cit.*, pp. 178 ff. On my own reconstruction of Hebrew phonology in the time of Origen (and the Dead Sea Scrolls) see *Archivum Linguisticum* 17 (1969), pp. 146 ff.

(Ps. lxxi 9) [1]). Must we transcribe this as [leʿeṯ], and deduce that the dialect behind the Palestinian texts had no murmured vowel sound, but reflects an earlier stage in the development of Hebrew when like Arabic it maintained full vowels in unstressed open syllables? I believe not. There is a much simpler explanation than that. The Palestinian vocalizers had the same view of language as their Tiberian successors, but they approached their task rather more frugally, being content most of the while with partial vocalizations; on the few occasions therefore that they felt it necessary to mark a murmured vowel sound, they did it in the only way open to them, namely by using a full vowel sign. But there is more to be said yet. It is possible to find the same device in the Tiberian system. I refer here not only to the [páṯaḥ] 'furtive' in מָשִׁיחַ etc., but to forms like מֶלֶךְ and similar so-called 'Segholates', and to a form like וַיַּעַזְבֵנִי 'he left me behind' (1 Sam. xxx 13), in which in the environment of the pharyngal there are two [páṯaḥ] signs, where in a corresponding regular verbal form there would be a closed syllable. The second [s^{e}gól] and [páṯaḥ] in these forms stand really for a [š^{e}wå′ nå′ḏ], and they should strictly speaking also be transcribed with raised [^{e,a}], מֶלֶךְ as [mέl^{e}ḵ] rather than /mέlɛk/ and יַעַזְבֵנִי as [ya^{a}z^{e}ḇéni] rather than /yaʿazĕbéni/. The syllabic structures are respectively CVCC (not CV + CVC) and CV^{e}+ CCV (not CV + CV + CCV + CV).

The other matter on which I wish to take issue with Morag is his treatment of the [dågéš] sign, which you will remember, he said had, like [š^{e}wå′], a two-fold function, first in the doubling of consonants and second in indicating the plosive over against the fricative alternatives of the *Beghadhkephath* sounds. Here Morag is in essence following the traditional grammarians, Jewish and European [2]), but

---

1) Cited from R. Meyer, *Hebräisches Textbuch* (Berlin 1960), p. 72. Graphically, the form is [leʿɛṯ], but the Palestinian equivalents of [s^{e}gól] and [ṣeré] (and of [påṯaḥ] and [qå′mɛṣ]) are interchangeable, showing that the dialect possessed only one [e] vowel and one [a] vowel, though at the time the system was formulated, each of these signs must have had a phonetic counterpart. For the latest information and bibliography on the Palestinian system see E. J. Revell, *Hebrew Texts with Palestinian Vocalization* (Toronto 1970).

2) For a full account of this nature, using (but sometimes criticizing) the very complicated Latin terminology, see F. R. Blake, 'The Origin and Development of the Hebrew Daghesh', *Journal of Biblical Literature* 62 (1943), pp. 89-107. The division into *forte* (חָזָק) and *lene* (קַל) goes back to the Jewish grammarians, who also occasionally

again, in faithfulness to the Tiberian Massoretes, I would argue that the sign was intended by them to mark only one feature, and further that this feature was a distributional not a phonetic one. We might see what was in their minds more clearly if, as they ought to have done, our modern editions of the Hebrew Bible printed the [råp̄ɛ] strokes as they are found in the mediaeval manuscripts instead of discarding them as redundant, and more clearly still if we took into our reckoning the peculiar vocalization of the *Codex Reuchlinianus*. The system used in this *Codex* has been variously identified as Ben Naphtali, proto-Tiberian and (although it employs the Tiberian signs) 'complicated' or 'fuller' Palestinian [1]), but we can, I think, safely ignore that problem as outwith the concern of this paper.

In Tiberian manuscripts every *Beghadhkephath* letter that begins a self-contained phrase or phonetic group or that directly follows a previous consonant is given a [dåg̱éš] point; every other *Beghadhkephath* letter is supplied with a [råp̄ɛ] stroke, whether it follows a full vowel or merely a [šᵉwå' nå'ḏ]. In this definition I have intentionally used the term 'phrase' or 'group', because it covers those frequent cases in which a *Beghadhkephath* letter in word initial position has [råp̄ɛ], where the previous word ends in a vowel. The one exception is cases like מַלְכֵי mentioned previously, where the כ after a [šᵉwå' nå'ḥ] is given [råp̄ɛ]. I shall come back to this awkward customer shortly, but meanwhile I cite a short passage from *Codex Reuchlinianus* (1 Sam. xxxi 6) [2])

וַיָּמָת שָׁאוּל וּשְׁלֹשֶׁת בָּנָיו וְנֹשֵׂא כֵלָיו וְגַם כָּל אֲנָשָׁיו בַּיּוֹם הַהוּא יַחְדָּו

use phrases like 'to beautify the reading' (דגש לתפארת הקריאה; *David Ḳimḥi's Hebrew Grammar*, § 16a) but the full classification into *necessarium*, *euphonicum*, *orthographicum*, *dirimens* etc., is due to later European ingenuity. On the argument of this paper all these terms are superfluous and misleading.

1) P. Kahle, *Massoreten des Westens* II (Stuttgart 1930), pp. 55*ff.; S. Morag, 'The Vocalization of Codex Reuchlinianus : Is the Pre-Masoretic Bible Pre-Masoretic ?', *Journal of Semitic Studies 4* (1959), pp. 216-37; S. Morag, *op. cit.* (*The Vocalization Systems* etc.), p. 38; A. Díez-Macho, 'A new list of so-called Ben Naftali MSS, preceded by an enquiry into the true character of these manuscripts', *Hebrew and Semitic Studies presented to G.R. Driver* (Oxford 1963), pp. 16-52; R. Meyer, 'Die Bedeutung des Codex Reuchlinianus für die hebräische Sprachgeschichte : Dargestellt aus Dageš-Gebrauch', *Zeitschrift des deutschen Morgenländische Gesellschaft* 113 (1963), pp. 51-61. On the problems of this *Codex* I have benefited from discussions with a former student, Mr J. D. Alexander, now of St. John's College, Oxford.

2) From A. Sperber, *A Historical Grammar*, p. 557 (as corrected by Mr Alexander from a facsimile). Sperber's rather despairing conclusions on this *Codex* (p. 559) should, in my view, not be accepted.

The point to notice is that [dåg̱éš] and [råp̱ɛ́] are used with nearly all the other letters in a manner almost exactly paralleling their use in Tiberian manuscripts with *Begadhkephath* letters; and the use is manifestly distributional, since the pronunciation of these letters cannot be in doubt. The cases where the parallel is not exact, notably the ל with [dåg̱éš] in ושלשת and the ד in יחדו, are particularly instructive; in the Tiberian system a *Beghadhkephath* letter in the position of ל would have a [råp̱ɛ́] stroke, and (assuming the different vowel) so equally would the ד.

The question we have to ask is, therefore : Was the original function of [dåg̱éš] and [råp̱ɛ́] to denote different pronunciations of certain consonants, a function that was then transferred to the graphic sphere by the scribe of *Codex Reuchlinianus* and extended through a false analogy to other letters? [1]) Or does *Codex Reuchlinianus*, though later than our earliest Ben Asher manuscripts, reflect an older stage in the usage of [dåg̱éš] and [råp̱ɛ́] than they do? Did, in other words, the Tiberian schoolmen restrict these signs to the *Beghadhkephath* letters, because only in their case was a phonetic factor involved in addition to the distributional one? If the second answer is the correct one, then the presence of [råp̱ɛ́] over the כ of מלכי would be the result of a false analogy—the phonetic one—working within the Tiberian system.

I am myself inclined to accept the second answer, but we have still to see how it fits in with the other chief use of [dåg̱éš], namely to indicate doubled consonants. Some scholars have argued that this use is the primary one, and the use in certain *Beghadhkephath* letters a secondary one, because like a geminate *Beghadhkephath* the sounds they represent are always plosive. The gravest weakness of this view is that it leaves the [råp̱ɛ́] sign hanging in the air, as it were, a mere afterthought of the vocalizers and not at all an equal partner of the [dåg̱éš]. Can we then find a distributional factor in the phonetic feature of gemination that would connect it with the distributional function which the second answer assumes was original in the case of non-geminate letters? I think we can; gemination like *zero* in its various guises is in Hebrew phonological (as distinct from morphological) structure essentially a link between syllables; a geminate consonant both ends a prior syllable

---

1) This is in essence the view of MORAG, *op. cit.*, pp. 38 ff., though he correctly describes the usage in *Codex Reuchlinianus*.

and begins a subsequent one, and it may have been because of this role that the Massoretes marked it in writing with a [dåg̱éš]. But even if the first answer is for the Tiberian system the right one, namely that the [dåg̱éš] (and at a later stage the [råp̄é]) originated to represent static phonetic features [1]) and not moving syllabic ones, we still have the irrefutable evidence from *Codex Reuchlinianus* that at least some Massoretes thought of the two signs as distributional in function. For the purpose of this paper that evidence is almost, if not quite as welcome.

It is time now to draw some general conclusions from my arguments. In an article published in 1969 in the periodical *Archivum Linguisticum* [2]) I stated my agreement with the view of I. J. GELB and others [3]) that the Semitic unpointed script is syllabic in character, each letter representing the unit of consonant plus any or no vowel. In addition to this basic function, three of the letters (הוי) denoted the internal 'prosodies' of [^{w,y}] (the phonemic diphthongs) and the final 'prosodies' of [^{w,y,h}] (the *matres lectionis*). In this statement I was using 'prosody' not in its restricted modern sense of to do with syllabic quantity and accentuation, particularly in poetry, though these matters are certainly included, but in a wider sense akin to that of the original Greek προσῳδία, a term that referred to the rough and smooth breathings as well as the system of accents. I drew attention to the dissatisfaction presently being voiced among phonologists, especially in Great Britain, with what they called a 'phoneme-dominated' phonology, and suggested that they may find allies in the inventors of the Semitic orthog-

[1]) The Hebrew (or Hebraized Aramaic) names of the two terms have sometimes been erroneously appealed to in justification of this traditional view; but it is most unlikely that they refer to the nature of the sounds as 'hard' and 'soft'. The name [dåg̱éš] is a participal form from the root DGŠ, which in Syriac means 'to stab, pierce', so it probably simply describes the dot itself, which 'pierces' a letter. The name [råp̄é] means 'weak' (not 'soft'), and could theoretically indicate the pronunciation of the *Beghadhkephath* consonants, if we considered a fricative sound to be in any phonetic sense 'weaker' than a plosive; but it could also be taken to refer to the position, and be rendered 'less prominent'.

[2]) 'On the Linguistic Analysis of Hebrew Writing', *Archivum Linguisticum* 17 (1969), pp. 131-60, especially pp. 154 ff. The examples used were taken from the Dead Sea Isaiah A scroll and from one of the Lachish Letters. See also my *Textbook of Syrian Semitic Inscriptions, I, Hebrew and Moabite Inscriptions* (Oxford 1971), pp. 34, 86.

[3]) I. J. GELB, *A Study of Writing* (Phoenix Books, Chicago, 1963), pp. 122 ff., especially 138 ff.; T. F. MITCHELL, *Writing Arabic* (OUP, 1953), pp. 14 ff.

raphy [1]). Just as the inventors of the first alphabets properly so-called, the Greek and even more the Latin (for the Greeks retained prosodies, whereas the Romans did not express accents and turned the rough breathing into a letter 'h'), may be named incipient 'phonemicists', so the Phoenician inventors and later Hebrew, Aramaean and Arab adaptors of the Semitic script may with equal justice be named incipient 'prosodists'.

I believe that the Tiberian and other Massoretes inherited from the scribes and Rabbis who handed down the biblical text a similar outlook on language. The primary purpose of the various vocalization systems (and we should include here the systems of accents) was to give in a period when the Hebrew language was no longer in everyday use as much information as possible about how the scriptures were to be read and pronounced. The signs, which were inserted as diacritics above, below and within the letters of the older orthography fulfilled two chief functions :

a. they supplied an indication of the vowel already implied in these letters, and where there was none, one of the signs was added to make this clear. As Gelb has already stressed—and in my view it is a very persuasive argument—if the unpointed letters simply stood for consonants, there would be no need for such a sign as the [š^{e}wå'], or in Arabic writing for the [sukuun].

b. they denoted *προσῳδίαι* of various kinds that the Massoretes felt would, if marked, help the reader of the Bible in the *continuous* pronunciation of the language. In other words, the Massoretes thought it just as important to indicate the *movement* of language as to split it up into its most convenient smallest parts, to indicate which syllables were prominent and which not, the different stresses and tones that operated in poetry and prose, when larger phonological units like feet and groups and phrases began and ended, what happened to consonants and vowels in certain positions, and so on. Marks for such features are notoriously lacking in alphabetic European writing in general and in English writing in particular, where spelling and punctuation have often little or no connection with pronunciation. In this paper I have

---

1) See in particular J. R. Firth, 'Sounds and Prosodies', *Transactions of the Philological Society*, 1948, pp. 127-52, reprinted in *Papers in Linguistics* 1934-1951 (OUP, 1957), pp. 121-38, and for a short account of the kind of techniques being adopted in 'prosodic' analysis, R. H. Robins, *General Linguistics : An Introductory Survey* (London 1964), pp. 157 ff.

concentrated in particular on the [šᵉwå'] and [ḥåṭép̱] signs, and on the [dåg̱éš] point and [råp̱ɛ́] stroke, and given my own view that their roles, if properly understood, entitle them to be called prosodic markers. If in describing that view I have castigated *both* the traditional Jewish and the later European grammarians with their Latinate categories *and* modern phonemic phonologists like Morag with their concern for linear transcription, it is because I am convinced that the techniques of neither bring us near the heart of the matter. The misunderstandings of many centuries have to be peeled away before we catch a glimpse of the Massoretes as linguistic thinkers. For all the jibes that have been levelled at them by those who in their ignorance have weighed these old Jewish philologists in the balance and found them wanting, I would claim that they still have a thing or two to teach us.

THE TRIBES IN THE BLESSING OF MOSES

BY

C. J. LABUSCHAGNE

Groningen

In its present context the so-called Blessing of Moses in Deut. xxxiii is an integral part of the series of concluding addresses delivered by Moses before his death. Although the chapters xxxi 1—xxxiii 29 consist of various passages, for the greater part concluding speeches, they form one coherent composition on the theme : the final arrangements made by Moses before his death. As I have tried to show elsewhere [1], the framework to the so-called Song of Moses is the whole series of concluding speeches, into which the Song has been incorporated, in such a way, however, that it cannot be lifted from its context and studied regardless of this framework. I do not believe that these chapters should be seen as late appendices to the book of Deuteronomy, because I consider the Deuteronomist(s) to be responsible for the entire montage of final addresses, including the Blessing of Moses. In comparison with the Song, which is intimately interwoven with its context, the Blessing can relatively easily be lifted from its present context, but this does not mean that it can be studied regardless of this specific context. As a matter of fact I think there is reason to believe that the Blessing consists of different elements, arranged and adapted in such a way that these elements together with newly composed parts constitute a poem designed for a specific purpose. The object of this poem is to let Moses pronounce before his death a eulogy on Israel as a nation and to praise Yahweh on the eve of the great moment when Israel took possession of the land given to it by Yahweh. With this aim in view the poem was given the function of a death-bed speech. In general character this poetic composition resembles the patriarchal death-bed speeches [2], more specifically those of Jacob in Gen. xlviii

---

[1]) C. J. Labuschagne, "The Song of Moses : Its framework and structure", *De fructu Oris Sui, Essays in honour of Adrianus Van Selms, Pretoria Oriental Series*, Vol. IX, Leiden 1971, pp. 85-98.

[2]) Cf. Gen. xxvii 27 ff.; xxviii 1 ff.; xlviii 3 ff.; xlviii 15 ff.; xlix 1 ff.

and xlix. The Blessing of Moses in Deut. xxxiii should not be compared with The Blessing of Jacob in Gen. xlix only, but also with Gen. xlviii. The tribal blessings in Deut. xxxiii resemble the tribal blessings in Gen. xlix, but the poem in Deut. xxxiii as a whole contains elements not to be found in Gen. xlix (which is a collection of tribal sayings). One of these elements is the element of acknowledging God's guidance. This element, which is an integral part of the death-bed speech, figures very prominently in the hymn-like framework to the tribal blessings in Deut. xxxiii, *i.e.* in the verses 2-5 and 26-29, but is found to be lacking in the collection of tribal sayings in Gen. xlix; it is part and parcel, however, of the death-bed speech delivered by Jacob in Gen. xlviii 3 ff. and 15 ff.

The principal difference between Gen. xlix and Deut. xxxiii is that the former is a collection of tribal sayings aimed at expressing the unity of the tribes among which the tribe of Judah is pre-eminent [1]), while the latter is a poem consisting of a hymnal part celebrating God's guidance, and a number of sayings concerning the tribes, the aim of which is to state the position of the tribes in the land given to them by Yahweh, who came with his people from the Sinai to the gateway to the promised land [2]), and who continues his protecting care for his people in Canaan. Another difference is that the Blessing of Jacob sees Israel from a southern point of view, while the Blessing of Moses offers an insight in Israel's self-understanding from a northern point of view. It is important to notice that while we may safely call the Blessing of Jacob a *collection* of sayings concerning the tribes, the Blessing of Moses can only partly so be called. As we shall see, the blessings given to the tribes of Reuben, Judah and Levi cannot possibly be labelled 'tribal sayings' (*Stammessprüche*), so that only the blessings given to the northern tribes may be called a collection of tribal sayings, should they so be labelled. I am afraid that the Blessing of Moses has often too rashly been regarded as a collection of tribal sayings, which scholars thought could be lifted from its hymn-like framework and studied regardless of these parts of the Blessing. It must be stressed, I think, that, compared with the Blessing of Jacob, which is indeed a collection of tribal sayings, the Blessing of Moses is a

---

[1]) See B. J. van der Merwe, "Judah in the Pentateuch", *Theologia Evangelica*, I (1968) pp. 37-52.

[2]) Cf. R. Tournay, "Le Psaume et les Bénédictions de Moïse", *RB* 65 (1958) pp. 181—213, especially p. 183.

poem, some component parts of which consist of tribal sayings. In addition to this, it is most important to notice that the blessings concerning the tribes in Deut. xxxiii are arranged in an order differing significantly from the tribal scheme in Gen. xlix, where we have the normative clan system. One of the aims of this paper is to offer an explanation of this remarkable scheme of clan affiliation. In order to do so we have to recognize that there is a more intimate connection between the tribal blessings and their hymn-like framework than we have so far been prepared to accept. Therefore I shall begin our discussion of the problem of the tribes by making a few remarks on the character of this framework and the relation between it and the tribal blessings. The first part of the hymn-like section of our poem, which is the most difficult, vss. 2-5, can be rendered as follows :

2. Yahweh came from Sinai, and He beamed forth from Seir for them, He shone forth from mount Paran, and came from Meribath-Kadesh [1]), at his right hand the slopes of Moab [2]).
3. A father [3]), who loves the people [4]), all his holy ones are at his/thy side [5]), they crouch at thy feet, they carry out thy decisions.
4. He commanded them [6]) the law, a possession [7]) for the assembly of Jacob.
5. Then He became King in Jeshurun, when the chiefs of the people were gathered, a unity the tribes of Israel.

The poem begins with a description of the purposive journey of Yahweh, accompanied by his people, from mount Sinai along the route over Paran and Kadesh to the slopes of the Pisgah at the gateway to Canaan. It is not a theophany our poet is describing, but he uses terms and motifs that belong to the theophany in his description of Yahweh's

---

1) See *BH*.

2) I propose to read *'ašdōt lᵉmô'āb*.

3) The reading *'āb* depends upon the conjecture at the end of verse 2, see *BH*.

4) In this context *ᶜammîm* denotes the Israelite tribes; cf. Gen. xxviii 3; xlviii 4 and Deut. xxxiii 19.

5) There is a change form the third person in the first half of the verse to the second person in the second half. It is difficult to decide whether we should read 'his side' or 'thy side'.

6) The subject of the verb is still Yahweh. The reading *mōšèh* is wrong; *lānu* is to be read *lāmô*.

7) This word does not refer to the law, but to the land, Cf. the remark by B. LINDARS, "Torah in Deuteronomy", *Words and Meanings, Essays presented to David Winton Thomas*, Cambridge 1968, p. 133 note 2. Cf. Ex. vi 8; Ez. xi 15; xxxiii 24.

coming with his people to their land : Yahweh comes [1]), shines forth, accompanied by the holy ones. It is not impossible of course that an older form of this poem was indeed a description of a theophany, and the reconstruction of these verses by CROSS and FREEDMAN [2]) can be seen as an attempt to reconstruct a description of a theophany. If so, these verses are in their present form an *Umdeutung* of an original theophany : Yahweh does not shine forth at Sinai, as in a theophany, but departs from Sinai on his way to Canaan; He is not accompanied by his angels, as in a theophany, but by his people, who are called 'his holy ones' [3]). The terms and motifs, adopted from the wordfield of the theophany, are given a new function, which is to describe the whole series of God's deeds of salvation : He takes decisive steps in the interest of his people, leads them through the desert to the very threshold of Canaan, loves them and makes them obedient, gives them the law [4]), becomes their king, and finally gives them their land [5]). There is no reason to doubt that the verses 26-29 constitute the second part of the hymn-like framework. Here Yahweh is praised as the incomparable One and Israel eulogized as a nation that dwells in security, an incomparable people because of the saving acts of its God, who drove away its enemies and gave it a good land. It is not unreasonable to think that these two parts originally belonged together [6]) and that the hymn was split in two precisely at the point where the 'tribes of Israel' are mentioned (vs. 5) [7]) in order to insert the tribal blessings. However, it should not be impossible either to imagine that this part of the poem was composed at the same time as the sayings concerning the tribes were arranged, adapted and recomposed or even composed to get their present form and to fit into the scheme as we have them now. As we cannot discuss this problem in any detail here, it must suffice to state the possibility. It doesn't make any difference really whether the various blessings were inserted in an existing hymn, or whether a hymn was composed for the purpose of giving the blessings a framework.

---

[1]) Cf. E. JENNI, "'Kommen' im theologischen Sprachgebrauch des Alten Testaments", *Wort, Gebot, Glaube* (*Festschrift für* W. EICHRODT) 1970, p. 256.

[2]) "The Blessing of Moses", *JBL* 67 (1948) pp. 202 f.

[3]) Cf. Ex. xix 6; Deut. vii 6; xiv 2, 21; xxvi 19; xxviii 9 and Jer. ii 3.

[4]) Unless this part of the verse is a gloss, see B. LINDARS, *op. cit.*, p. 133.

[5]) See E. JENNI, *op. cit.*, p. 256.

[6]) Cf. I. L. SEELIGMANN, "A psalm from pre-regal times", *VT* 14 (1964) pp. 75-92; and TH. H. GASTER, *JBL* 66 (1947) pp. 53-62.

[7]) See SEELIGMANN, *op. cit.*, pp. 76, 78 and 83 ff.

What is important is that the Blessing of Moses connects the fact of Israel being settled as a nation in Canaan with the Sinai event. The very fact that the Sinai tradition of a covenant relationship is so intimately linked with Yahweh's rule in Israel at that point in history when the tribes became a nation and settled in their own land, is not only significant in itself, but also shows that Israel's consciousness of itself as a nation is connected with a pre-settlement event. The fact that the sayings concerning the tribes were put into a framework celebrating the felicity of the nation as a whole, secured to it by Yahweh through the Sinai covenant relationship, proves that one should not look for the origins of Israel's unity elsewhere than in the institution of the Sinai covenant [1]). There is evidence to show that both the hymn-like framework and the sayings concerning the individual tribes, excepting one (Levi), date from a very early period : the time of the judges and, in my opinion, not later than the first years of the rule of David [2]). So far as the connection between the blessings and their framework is concerned, one might base an argument on the value one might attach to the superscription. I am not sure whether it is wise in this case to regard the superscription as what we are wont to call a 'redactional note'. Considering that the term 'man of God' does not occur elsewhere in the Pentateuch, but six times referring to Moses, e.g. in Ps. xc [3]), we have reason to believe that this term was not invented by the Deuteronomist, but that it was part of an existing superscription belonging to the poem and taken over by the Deuteronomist when he made his montage of Moses' concluding speeches.

The problem of the superscription brings us to the next stage in our discussion, the way in which the individual blessings are introduced in the poem and the way in which the tribes are arranged. Looking at the introduction formulae, we see that the Reuben-blessing has no introduction whatsoever, and that the phrase introducing the Judah-blessing, 'and this concerning Judah, and he said', is not only awkward but it also differs significantly from the fixed formula used to introduce the rest of the blessings. We also notice —and this is something that

---

[1]) Cf. G. W. ANDERSON, "Israel : Amphictyony : ᶜam; kāhāl; ᶜedâh", *Translating and understanding the Old Testament, Essays in honor of H. G. MAY*, New York 1970, pp. 135-151, especially p. 150.

[2]) See CROSS and FREEDMAN, *op. cit.*, p. 192, and see further below.

[3]) Cf. A. VAN SELMS, "Die uitdrukking "Man van God" in die Bybel", *Hervormde Teologiese Studies* 15 (1959) pp. 133-149.

seems to have escaped the notice of all commentators—that the Levi-blessing is introduced by the words '*and* of Levi he said' while the formula introducing the Benjamin-blessing lacks the connecting 'and' for it reads 'of Benjamin he said'. All the rest of the blessings following after the Benjamin-blessing are introduced by the formula 'and of... he said' [1]). If we assume, and to me there seems no reason for doubt, that these introduction formulae are not simply 'redactional notes', but that they are at least as old as the poem, these facts concerning the way in which the individual blessings are introduced, can be used as additional evidence to show that the sayings concerning the northern tribes (Benjamin, Joseph, etc.) constituted a separate and disticnt group, that may be called a collection of eulogistic tribal sayings. On the other hand, the phrases introducing the blessings concerning the southern tribes indicate that these blessings belong to a different category and perhaps also date from a different time, as I hope to show presently on the strength of the internal evidence coming from the blessings themselves. The Judah-blessing and the Reuben-blessing, compared with the blessings concerning the northern tribes, belong to the same category, *viz.* that of a wish or intercessory prayer, which makes it very probable that they were introduced by identical formulae. It is almost certain that the phrase introducing the Reuben-blessing was : *zō't habb*ᵉ*rākāh lir*ᵉ*'ubēn* 'this is the blessing for Reuben', which explains the meaning of the awkward phrase introducing the Judah-blessing : 'and this is it (i.e. the blessing) for Judah'. The Levi-blessing, in a very special way inserted in the Judah blessing, as we shall see, has an introduction formula similar to that used in connection with the northern tribes, but is quite out of place with respect to them. Its type resembles that of the Judah-blessing in so far as in both of them God is addressed in the second person, contradistinguishing them from the northern blessings where Yahweh is spoken of in the third person. Before discussing the blessings concerning the southern tribes individually, let us first turn to the problem of the remarkable order in which the tribes are arranged.

It has often been noticed, that we have in Deut. xxxiii a completely different order of the tribes compared with the normal, or more customary scheme of clan affiliation, to be found, e.g. in Gen xlix. Simeon is lacking, Judah is mentioned before Levi [2]), Benjamin precedes

---

1) These differences are thoroughly obscured e.g. in the New English Bible.

2) The only other instance is in Ez. xlviii.

Joseph [1]), while the order of the six most northern tribes occurs nowhere else. Some scholars think that the order of the tribes shows a lack of any logical scheme [2]), and H.-J. ZOBEL has drawn the conclusion that the collection of sayings in Deut. xxxiii must be older than that in Gen. xlix, because it lacks the later, normative scheme of clan affiliation [3]). C. ARMERDING [4]) on the other hand, has tried to show that, compared with the order in Gen. xlix, the tribes are here arranged from Judah onwards in pairs, and that the order of names in each pair has been inverted. However, this is only partly true, for in both Gen. xlix and Deut. xxxiii (and also in Jud. v) Zebulon precedes Issachar, while they occur elsewhere in the opposite order. In addition to this it has to be noticed that in Gen. xlix the sons of Rachel are mentionned at the end of the list, while in Deut. xxxiii they follow Levi, or more correctly, Judah. ARMERDING has not explained for what reason such a supposed device of inverting the order of the pairs was employed. An objection to his view is, that, if the order of the pairs in Deut. xxxiii is the opposite of that in Gen. xlix, then the scheme of clan affiliation in Deut. xxxiii must presuppose the scheme in Gen. xlix which it obviously does not. I think that the key for solving the problem of the order of the tribes in the Blessing of Moses can be found by looking at the map. In the first part of the poem, (vss. 2-5), we can see that there is a tendency to indicate a moving from south to north, more specifically from mount Sinai to mount Pisgah in Moab, the gateway to Canaan : Yahweh comes from Sinai, from Paran, from Meribath-Kadesh up north until the slopes of Moab, i.e. the slopes of mount Pisgah, are at his right hand, which can only mean that He is at that stage supposed to be facing west. Starting from that point in Moab and crossing the Jordan, one can clearly see that the order of the tribes can be described as a journey through their territory, which is quite obvious at least so far as the first tribes are concerned : Reuben east of the Jordan, then Judah on the other side, then moving north one passes through Benjamin in order to arrive in the territory of Joseph. Leaving the problem of the

---

1) Also in Num. xxxiv and Jud. i.

2) See H.-J. ZOBEL. "Die Stammessprüche des Mose-Segens (Dnt. 33,6-25)", *Klio* 46 (1965), p. 87, and recently also C. H. J. DE GEUS, *De stammen van Israël*, Groningen 1972, p. 70.

3) H.-J. ZOBEL, *op. cit.*, p. 87.

4) C. ARMERDING, "The last words of Moses : Deuteronomy 33", *Bibliotheca Sacra* 114 (1957) pp. 225-234, especially p. 227.

'lost' tribe of Simeon for a moment, and postponing the problem of Levi for a while, we can state that we are now able to see why Benjamin is mentioned after Judah (and Levi, who had no territory !) and before Joseph [1]). The route from Sinai to the slopes of the Pisgah, which Yahweh came with his people, is now being continued in the route through the territories of the tribes. Thus it becomes clear that the different order of the tribes in Deut. xxxiii is determined by geographical factors, and not by genealogical ones as in Gen. xlix (the sons of Leah, the sons of the two slave-women, the sons of Rachel). This geographical factor is also operative in the order of the six most northern tribes. They are arranged in the following order : Zebulon, Issachar, Gad, Dan, Naphtali, Asher. This remarkable order can be explained as follows : if we take a point somewhere west of the sea of Galilee as our centre, and then describe a circle in an anti-clockwise direction starting in the territory of Zebulon, we pass through the territories of these tribes in the very order in which they are arranged here. They constitute what we may call the Northern Circle, for they belong together in a special way, either affiliated in a league of clans, or perhaps even united in something like an amphictyony, the centre of which may most probably have been mount Tabor [2]). This situation obviously reflects an earlier phase of tribal history, before the arrival of the Rachel group, but we cannot go into this question here, as it is not the aim of the present paper to study tribal origins. Summing up our conclusion we can say that the order of the tribes in Deut. xxxiii is not determined by genealogical, but by geographical factors : they are mentioned in the order as one meets them when one follows the route we described, and the object of the poet who arranged the blessings in this particular order, must have been to stress the idea of the occupation of the land, or better the unity of the tribes settled in Canaan.

Having thus found a solution to the problem of the order of the tribes, we can now pay attention to the problems concerning the individual tribes, more specifically the southern tribes. First, there is the problem of the complete silence respecting the tribe of Simeon. The absence of a blessing for Simeon cannot be explained in any satisfactory way by

---

1) Cf. M. NOTH, *Das System der zwölf Stämme Israels*, 1930, repr. 1966, p. 22.

2) See G. VON RAD, *Theologie des Alten Testaments*, I, München 1958², p. 30 (English translation, p. 21); H.-J. ZOBEL, *op. cit.*, p. 90; H.-J. KRAUS, *Gottesdienst in Israel*, München 1962², pp. 194-201 and S. HERRMANN, "Autonome Entwicklungen in den Königreichen Israel und Juda", *VT Suppl.* 17, p. 150.

assuming that it has been omitted accidentally. Nor can the explanation given by M. NOTH be accepted, that Simeon is lacking because the collector had no saying concerning this tribe at his disposal [1]). Such an answer to the question is unsatisfactory for two reasons. First, because, at least so far as the southern tribes are concerned, as we have seen, there is no reason to think in terms of a collection of tribal sayings where some unfortunate tribe runs the risk of being omitted by accident or because of its failure to provide the collector with a saying at the moment of collecting. Second, because NOTH has failed to recognize the historical circumstances reflected by the very fact of the absence of this particular tribe in this context. The situation presupposed by the composer of the Blessing of Moses is that of the individual tribes as they became settled, each in its own territory. This situation does not only effect the tribe of Levi, that had no territory of its own, but also the tribe of Simeon. The answer to the question of Simeon's absence, therefore, must be that this tribe had no territory of its own at the time of the composition of our poem. Whatever the original position of the tribe of Simeon might have been in earlier times [2]), it had obviously lost its individuality and had dwindled into insignificance at the time of the composition of the Blessing of Moses. It had been absorbed by the tribe of Judah. Gen. xlix 7 tells us that the tribe of Simeon together with the secular tribe of Levi, was dispersed in Israel. According to Jud. i 3, 17 this tribe accompanied the tribe of Judah on its campaign against the Canaanites, and Jos. xix 1,9 report that its inheritance formed part of the territory of Judah [3]). Whatever significance this tribe might have had as a separate entity in the far south of the territory of Judah, to our poet it had ceased to mean anything as a separate tribe [4]). The only possible trace of Simeon in the mind of the composer of our poem is a word-play on the name of this tribe in the word *š*^{e}*ma*^{c}, the first word of the Judah-blessing, but even this is far from certain.

---

[1]) M. NOTH, *op. cit.*, p. 22.

[2]) Cf. Gen. xxxiv where it is supposed that this tribe together with Levi once lived in central Palestine.

[3]) See R. DE VAUX, "The Settlement of the Israelites in Southern Palestine and the Origins of the Tribe of Judah", *Translating and understanding the Old Testament, Essays in honor of H. G. May*, New York 1970, pp. 108-134, more particularly pp. 112 ff. and 132.

[4]) In Num. xxvi the tribe of Simeon is the smallest with 22,200. Codex A and other mss. of the LXX insert Simeon in verse 6b, but this is evidently a correction: see S. R. DRIVER, *Deuteronomy (ICC)*, Edinburgh 1902², p. 395.

The Reuben-blessing opens the series of blessings, not because the tribe of Reuben had any pre-eminence here, as the eldest of the brothers, but because of the geographical position of its territory, as we have tried to show. Compared with the Blessing of Jacob, where the pre-eminence of Reuben is most adequately recognized, the Blessing of Moses does not even mention the possibility of a primacy of this tribe, but goes no further than expressing a friendly wish for the bare existence of Reuben as a tribe. Of all the attempts to render the Reuben-blessing the following translation is the most plausible :

May Reuben live and not die ! But as for his men, may he be few ! [1])

If the verbal form *wîhî* in the second part of the verse is a jussive, what it obviously and naturally is seeing that it is preceded by two jussives, then we have to take the *waw* in an adversative sense and render it 'but', in order to get a translation that makes any sense. This means that the wish for Reuben's welfare is qualified and so to speak limited to moderate proportions. In view of the fact that the LXX renders the verse so as to make it an unqualified wish : '... and let him be *many* in number', and because scholars seem to find it difficult to accept the idea of a qualified or limited wish [2]), it has been suggested to take the form *wîhî* not as a jussive, but as a shortened imperfect, and to translate : 'Let Reuben live and not die so that his men be few' i.e. in the sense 'let him not die with the result that his men become few' [3]). But so far as I could see, there is not a single instance in the Old Testament where *wîhî* expresses the result of an action indicated by a jussive preceding it; after a jussive *wîhî* always expresses an additional wish [4]). I fail to see any reason why we should not accept the fact that the wish for the welfare of Reuben is a qualified

---

[1]) For this rendering, see below.

[2]) See *BH* and the commentaries.

[3]) So e.g. J. Ridderbos, *Het Boek Deuteronomium*, II (Korte Verklaring der Heilige Schrift) Kampen 1964², p. 124; G. von Rad, *Das fünfte Buch Mose: Deuteronomium* (*ATD*) Göttingen 1964, p. 144; C. Steuernagel, *Deuteronomium, Josua, Einleitung zum Hexateuch* (*Handkommentar zum A.T.*) Göttingen 1900, p. 124. The second part of the verse is rendered by H. Junker, *Das Buch Deuteronomium* (Die Heilige Schrift des Alten Testaments) Bonn 1933, p. 131, "wenn seiner Leute auch nur wenige sind".

[4]) See e.g. Gen. i 6; ix 27; Num. xxiii 10; Ps. lxxxi 16; xc 16 f.; Hos. xiv 7; 1 Sam. xviii 17c, 21; Ruth ii 12. Both Gesenius-Kautzsch-Cowley, *Hebrew Grammar*, par. 109h, and C. Brockelmann, *Syntax*, par. 135b misunderstood Ps. civ 20, where the first verbs are jussive forms in conditional sentences with the main clause in verse 20b—see P. Joüon, *Grammaire de l'Hébreu Biblique*, Rome 1965, par. 167.

one, especially in view of the fact that even in Gen. xlix, where Reuben's pre-eminence and his rights as the first-born are acknowledged, it is explicitly said : 'you shall *not* have pre-eminence' (vs.4). What the composer of the Reuben-blessing in Deut. xxxiii wanted to say is this : Reuben may continue existing as a tribe, but it should do so moderately, not striving after primacy among the tribes. In order to understand what precisely is meant by this qualified wish for the continuous existence of this tribe within moderate proportions, we must try to get a clear picture of the position of the tribe and the relation between it and the rest of the tribes, more specifically its relations with the two leading tribes, Judah and Joseph. Geographically Reuben occupied a special place among the tribes because it had its territory in the southern part of the transjordan area. To a certain extent it was isolated from Judah, but on the other hand it had definite connections with the northern tribes. In the Song of Deborah, e.g. Reuben is mentioned, while there is no reference whatsoever to the southern tribes of Judah and Simeon. Like Benjamin, Reuben [1]) was regarded as belonging to the tribes constituting Israel, in contradistinction with Judah and Simeon as the tribes that constitute Judah. Reuben's sympathies for the northern tribes are amply illustrated in the patriarchal narratives, e.g. in the conspiracy against Joseph (Gen. xxxvii 21 ff. and xlii 22) Reuben took Joseph's side and tried to save his life by suggesting that he be cast in the pit alive. This made him an opponent of Judah, who advised that Joseph be sold. Reuben's sympathy for Benjamin is clearly shown by his offer to guarantee the safe return of Benjamin at the risk of the life of his two sons (Gen. xlii 37). Reuben was Jacob's first-born only *de jure* (Gen. xxix 32; xxxv 23; xlvi 8; xlix 3; Ex. vi 13; Num. xxvi 5), for from the northern point of view this right *de facto* belonged to Joseph, *c.q.* to Joseph's two sons, whose adoption by Jacob amounted to giving Joseph a double portion of the inheritance, i.e. the equivalent of what the first-born was entitled to get [2]). This means that not Reuben, but Joseph was appointed successor of Jacob, and that he rose to a status equalling or even sur-

---

[1]) See B. ODDED, "The settlement of the tribe of Reuben in Transjordania", Studies in the History of the Jewish people and the land of Israel in memory of Zvi AVNERI, Haifa 1970, pp. 11-36; J. B. CURTIS, "Some suggestions concerning the history of the tribe of Reuben", *JBR* 23 (1965) pp. 247-250.

[2]) See B. J. VAN DER MERWE, "Joseph as successor of Jacob", *Studia Biblica et Semitica TH. C. VRIEZEN... dedicata,* Wageningen 1966, pp. 221-232, especially p. 226.

passing that of Reuben, so that he can be called 'the prince among his brothers' and likened to a first-born bull (Deut. xxxiii 16, 17). As for Reuben's relations with Judah we can state that Reuben was only *de jure* the leader among the brothers, for from the southern point of view it was *de facto* Judah who was the leader (Gen. xlix 8 ff.) [1]. In the Blessing of Jacob Reuben's loss of his pre-eminence is traced to the fact that he 'climbed into the bed of this father' (Gen. xlix 4; xxxv 22), a charge indicating that he tried to usurp power [2]. It is against this background that the Reuben-blessing must be interpreted. The very fact that the blessing expresses the wish that Reuben should have a moderate existence and not rise to a position of primacy, presupposes that there was danger that Reuben could do so. Now the question arises precisely when Reuben could have been in a position to regain its pre-eminence. The answer to this question can only be given after we have discussed the Judah-blessing, for these two blessings belong together and relate to the same historical situation. Without discussing in detail all difficulties regarding the Judah-blessing, I venture the following rendering:

7. And this is it for Judah. And he said:
Hear, O Yahweh, the cry of Judah, and wilt thou bring him to his people [3].
With thy hands fight for him [4], and be thou a help against his foes.
11. Bless, O Yahweh, his power, and wilt thou favour the work of his hands.
Smite his adversaries hip and thigh and those that hate him, that they rise no more.

For reasons to be given below, I consider verse 11 part of the Judah-blessing. One of the reasons is the form and style of this verse, which closely resembles that of verse 7. This prayer for the advantage of Judah consists of four lines, each of which has an imperative in the first half of the line, and a second person jussive in the second. Therefore the M.T. reading *yādāw rāb lô* should be emended to read *yādèkā rîb lô* in order to get the required imperative [5]. In any case, seeing the

---

[1] Cf. VAN DER MERWE, "Judah in the Pentateuch", *op. cit.*, pp. 37 ff.

[2] Cf. 2 Sam. xvi 21 f. (Absalom) and 1 Ki. ii 17 ff. (Adonijah); on the meaning of the taking possession of the harem, see A. VAN SELMS "Die oorname van 'n harem deur 'n nuwe koning", Hervormde Teol. Studies, 5 (1949) pp. 25-51.

[3] See, however, CROSS and FREEDMAN, *op. cit.*, pp. 193 and 203.

[4] For the various ways in which this part of the verse has been rendered, it might suffice here to refer the reader to the commentaries.

[5] See E. SELLIN, "Zu dem Judaspruch im Jaqobsegen Gen. 49,8-12", *ZAW* 60 (1944) p. 65; H. JUNKER, *op. cit.*, p. 131.

uncertainty as to the correct reading, I think one should not base any arguments on the doubtful words *yādāw rāb lô* in M.T., as DRIVER [1]) and ZOBEL [2]) and others [3]) have done, as evidence that Judah was engaged in contests for the common weal, which makes it a suitable candidate to apply for membership of the league of northern tribes, or that Judah fought for a reunion with the other tribes [4]). The Judah-blessing is a prayer in the interest of and for the advantage of this tribe. The fact that the hope is expressed that Judah be brought to 'its people' is evidence enough to show that the poet is obviously not a member of the tribe, but a north-Israelite, for the term *ᶜammô* is not very likely to mean anything else than the kindred tribes, which can only be the northern tribes [5]). The prayer clearly presupposes a situation in which Judah is not only isolated from the other tribes, but also in danger. In my opinion the opening words of the prayer 'Hear, O Yahweh, the voice of Judah' can only mean 'hear Judah's cry in distress, hearken to its cry for help', and I think ZOBEL [6]) is wrong when he renders *qôl* in German with '*Bitte*', taking it as referring to a request, supposed to have been made by Judah, to be accepted as a member of the league of northern tribes. The term *šᵉmaʿ qôl* is a *terminus technicus* used in prayer, in which *qôl* always connotes the cry for help addressed to God [7]), and therefore the word cannot refer here to a request addressed to humans. The important question is now : when was Judah in such a situation as presupposed, *i.e.* isolated from the rest of the tribes *and* in danger ? And when was Reuben at the same time in a position to re-establish its pre-eminence and its primacy over the other tribes ? It is always possible to venture speculations [8]), but there is indeed only one period in the history of Israel into which

---

1) S. R. DRIVER, *op. cit.*, p. 396.

2) H.-J. ZOBEL, *op. cit.*, p. 87; see also H.-J. ZOBEL, *Stammesspruch und Geschichte*, BZAW 95, Berlin 1965, p. 29.

3) See e.g. K. F. KRÄMER, *Numeri und Deuteronomium, Die Heilige Schrift für das Leben erklärt*, Freiburg 1955, p. 583.

4) J. RIDDERBOS, *op. cit.*, p. 128.

5) Some of the older commentators thought that the prayer was said for Judah when it went forth to battle and that 'his people' means Judah's own people at home; so e.g. KEIL, see DRIVER, *op. cit.*, p. 396.

6) H.-J. ZOBEL, *op. cit.* (*Stammesspruch*) pp. 28 f.

7) Cf. Ps. xxvii 7; xxviii 2; lxiv 2; cxix 149 (note also Ps. v 4; xviii 7 and cxvi 1 and the *t.t.* 'hear my prayer' Ps. iv 2; xxxix 13; liv 4; lxxxiv 9, etc.).

8) For differing views, see the commentaries.

this state of affairs fits precisely, and which meets all the requirements, and that is the time that David became king over Judah in Hebron. During those days Judah was isolated from the northern tribes, because the Philistines still occupied the whole area surrounding the Canaanite enclave of the Jerusalem region, for it was only afterwards that David drove them out of the valley of Rephaim and smote them from Geba to Gezer (2 Sam. v 17 ff., 25) [1]), which means that they still formed a threat to the new kingdom at that time, cutting it off from the rest of the tribes. At the same time Eshbaal, the son of Saul, became king in Transjordan out of the reach of the Philistines and claimed to rule all Israel, a claim which made him David's rival. There in Transjordan Eshbaal undoubtedly tried to rally the transjordan tribes to his side, more particularly the tribe of Reuben, to help him dethrone David. It is not impossible that the Reubenites were eager to do so, in order to regain their position of pre-eminence. This situation in which Judah began to emerge as vulnerable state constituting a separate entity within Israel to which Eshbaal in Transjordan laid claim, was a very dangerous one indeed and a threat to the unity of Israel. In my opinion it was the aim of the composer of our poem to avert this danger. This he did, on the one hand by stressing the unity of the promised land by means of the geographical principle according to which he arranged the tribes, and on the other hand by trying to close the ever widening gap between Judah and Israel, hoping sincerely that Judah could be reunited with its people, and by trying to prevent the Reubenites from realizing whatever claims they may have to primacy, hoping that Reuben would not raise an army and rally round Eshbaal against David. LINDBLOM has most convincingly shown [2]) that the political background of the so-called Shiloh-oracle in Gen. xlix 10 is this particular historical situation and that the oracle expresses the hope that Judah would extend its rule to Shiloh in order to comprise the northern tribes too. What has been expressed in the Blessing of Jacob from a southern point of view, concerning the unity of Israel : Judah as the leading tribe, destined to have primacy over all Israel is given in the Blessing of Moses as seen from a northern point of view : Judah should

---

[1]) See J. BRIGHT, *A History of Israel*, Philadelphia 1959, pp. 177 f.

[2]) J. LINDBLOM, "The political background of the Shiloh oracle", *VT Suppl.* I, Leiden 1953, pp. 78-87, more particularly pp. 84 ff. See also the important remarks by J. A. EMERTON. "Some difficult words in Genesis 49", *Words and Meanings, Essays presented to David Winton Thomas*, Cambridge 1968, pp. 81 ff. especially pp. 83-88.

be brought to its people, however not as the leading tribe, but as part of Israel, the league of tribes among which Joseph, the 'prince among his brothers' (Deut. xxxiii 16) is the leader. Another difference between the Blessing of Jacob and that of Moses is, that the latter is not so outspoken as the former when it comes to the primacy of one tribe over the others.

Having established the historical background against which the Reuben- and the Judah-blessing must be interpreted, and after what we have said with regard to the order of the tribes and the purpose of the composer, we can now see that the Levi-blessing does not fit into the poem. Its present position shows that it has been inserted in the Judah-blessing according to the literary device of split and insert [1]), probably by a levitical redactor who missed Levi among the tribes here. The name of Levi was omitted by the composer of our poem for the simple reason that the Levites had no territory of their own. In addition to evidence advanced by CROSS and FREEDMAN [2]) showing that the Levi-blessing is a later addition, we can state that there is strong evidence to show that, compared with the Blessing of Jacob (and Gen. xxxiv) where Levi denotes a secular tribe, the Blessing of Moses, or more correctly, the addition in it of a Levi-blessing, uses the name Levi to denote the Levites and not the tribe of Levi [3]). This is another reason for considering vs. 11 part of the Judah-blessing, because the contents of this verse clearly pertains to a tribe that has to fight for its existence, which can be said of Judah, but not of the Levites. Regarding the Levi-blessing as a later addition is the only way of explaining why this blessing appears out of place with respect to the two blessings for the southern tribes introduced by the formula 'this is the blessing for...', and also why this blessing appears out of place with respect to the collection of blessings pertaining to the northern tribes introduced by the formula 'of... he said'. As a matter of fact I think that the so-called Levi-blessing was inserted into the

---

1) Other instances are, e.g. Deut. xxxi 14-23, where the verses 16-22 have been inserted in the section consisting of verses 14, 15, 23; and e.g. Deut. xxvii 2-8, where the verses 4-7 have been inserted in the passage 2,3,8; and e.g. Zech. vi 9-14, where 12-13 (and 15) must be considered an insertion in the section 9,10,11,14 (VAN DER WOUDE in an oral communication).

2) CROSS and FREEDMAN, *op. cit.*, pp. 203 f.

3) For a discussion of the problems, see A. H. J. GUNNEWEG, *Leviten und Priester* (FRLANT 89) Göttingen 1965, pp. 37-81 and also now C. H. J. DE GEUS, *op. cit.*, pp. 74-84.

Judah-blessing without any phrase introducing it. The words *ûl^e^lēwî* *'āmar* are to be taken as part of the first line of the Levi-passage, where we miss a verb [1]). With a slight emendation, only a question of haplography, the beginning of this line reads as follows : *ûl^e^lēwî* *'āmartā tummèkā*... 'To Levi thou hast assigned thy Thummim, thy Urim to thy godly one' [2]). By inserting the Levi-passage so to speak in the heart of the Judah-blessing, our glossator, probably a refugee Levite who found a home in Judah, showed that the Levites had their spiritual home in Judah, a situation reflecting conditions after the fall of the northern kingdom, when many Levites fled to Judah.

To sum up : The blessings in Deut. xxxiii cannot be considered tribal sayings, nor can they be called a collection. One has to distinguish between the blessings concerning the southern tribes Reuben and Judah, and the northern tribes. The tribes are arranged according to a geographical principle, which explains their order here. The six tribes forming the northern circle belong together in a special way, and the blessings pertaining to them might have been an existing collection that might have had its original *Sitz im Leben* in some cultic festival or other celebrated on mount Tabor, the mountain referred to in verse 19, an event in which the tribes of Zebulon and Issachar played a leading rôle. The blessings pertaining to Benjamin and Joseph were added to the sayings concerning the six of the northern circle, which reflects a situation when the Rachel tribes were pre-eminent in the north with Joseph as the leader. The composition of the blessings pertaining to the southern tribes dates from the beginning of David's rule in Hebron, at which time the poem was composed as one of the finest examples of Israel's self-consciousness expressed in a poem.

---

[1]) The LXX translation 'Give Levi thy Urim' as well as the Quamran fragment *tèn l^e^* brought about a necessary correction by supplying a verb, but the verb does not fit the context, at least not in the imperative form.

[2]) For this connotation of *'amar l^e^* see 1 Ki. xi 18 and 2 Chr. xxix 24.

THE PROPHECY OF THE *YŌM YHWH* IN AMOS V 18-20

BY

C. VAN LEEUWEN

Utrecht

18 Woe unto you that long for the day of the Lord.
What will the day of the Lord mean to you?
It will be darkness, not light.
19 It will be as when a man flees from a lion
and a bear meets him,
and when he turns into his house and leans his hand on the wall
a snake bites him.
20 The day of the Lord indeed will be darkness, not light,
gloomy, without any brightness.

The masoretic text seems to be correct. There are only a few differences in the versions. LXX (cf. Vg.) takes *zè* in *lāmā-zè lākèm yōm yhwh* as a subject relating to *yōm* : ἵνα τί αὕτη ὑμῖν ἡ ἡμέρα τοῦ κυριοῦ; The Vg. connects this *yōm* with the following words : *Dies domini ista tenebrae et not lux* [1]). The word *zè* is here, however, not the subject of the sentence, but the intensification of the interrogative *lāmā*. Moreover, in vs. 20 the versions read the substantive *'ōfèl* (*γνόφος*, *caligo*) instead of the masoretical adjective *'āfēl*. The adjective forms, however, a good parallel to the phrase *w*^e^*lō-nōgah lō*, which is certainly meant as an adjectival addition to *yōm*.

Am. v 18-20 is one of the three woe-oracles in the book of Amos : v 7 (where the first words are probably to be read as *hōy hahōf*^e^*kīm*[2]), v 18 and vi 1. The particle *hōy* occurs in the O.T. in three different forms of usage : a) as a vocative appeal or address, e.g. Isa. xviii 1 : *hōy 'èrèṣ ṣilṣal k*^e^*nāfayim...*, 'Ho, land shadowing with wings, which is beyond the river of Cush.' b) as a mourning-cry, e.g. 1 Ki. xiii 30: He

---

[1]) The same connection in W. R. HARPER, *Amos and Hosea*, ICC, Edinburgh 1953, ad loc.; A. VAN HOONACKER, *Les douze petits prophètes*, Paris 1908, ad loc.

[2]) The omission of *hy* in M is explainable by the fact that a copyist wrote two in stead of three *h*'s.

laid the body in his own grave and they mourned for him, saying: *hōy 'āḥī*, 'alas my brother'; cf. *hō* in Am. v 16: There shall be wailing in every street and in all open places they shall say: 'alas, alas'. Usually, *hōy* is followed in these instances by a substantive indicating the relation of the mourning man or woman to the dead one. c) as the 'woe' in such prophetic indictments as we have got in Am. v 18. Generally, the *hōy*-words are grouped by the interpreters into these three different classes: mourning-cry, vocative appeal or address, and prophetic indictment. Besides, these classes would have to be considered as independent one on the other. Thus we read in an article of WANKE: "Ein auf den ersten Blick uneinheitlicheres Bild (als der Schreckruf *'ōy*) bietet das Wörtchen *hōy* mit seinen verschiedenen Bedeutungsnuancen, da es zunächst drie voneinander unabhängig scheinenden Bereichen zuzuordnen ist" [1]).

The "Sitz im Leben" of the prophetic woe has been looked for in very different spheres. MOWINCKEL [2]) thought it to be in the ritual of blessings and curses in the Israelite cult. The lists transmitting such curses (Deut. xxvii-xxviii) do not use, however, the particle *hōy*, but the participle *'ārūr*. Recently, GERSTENBERGER and WOLFF [3]) sought the "Sitz im Leben" of the prophetic *hōy*-oracle in Israelite wisdom: the prophetic *hōy* would have come into existence as the counterpart of *'ašrē*; the two words would originally have had a pedagogical function in popular ethics. To see the origin of the prophetic "woe" in wisdom is no more probable than seeing it in the cult of ancient Israel, first of all because *hōy* never occurs in the O.T. in parallelism with *'ašrē* and indeed never occurs in wisdom literature at all. There we find only the particle *'ōy*, the original cry of terror, generally—unlike *hōy*—constructed with *l*e + suffix, a difference that has almost been neglected by WOLFF. Moreover, LIPINSKI [4]) has shown that the statistics of *'ašrē* (26 from 45 O.T. instances occurring in the book of Psalms) point to the conclusion that *'ašrē*-words belong to the language of Psalms and do not find their origin in wisdom. According to WOLFF the wisdom-

---

1) G. WANKE, *'ōy* und *hōy*, *ZAW* 78 (1966), p. 217.

2) S. MOWINCKEL, *Psalmenstudien V. Segen und Fluch in Israels Kult und Psalmendichtung*, Oslo 1924. C. WESTERMANN (*Grundformen prophetischer Rede*, München 1960, p. 139 ff.) emphasizes also the connection between curse and prophetic woe oracle.

3) E. GERSTENBERGER, 'The woe oracles of the prophets', *JBL* 81 (1962), p. 249-263; H. W. WOLFF, *Amos' geistige Heimat*, Neukirchen 1964, p. 12-23.

4) E. LIPINSKI, 'Macarismes et Psaumes de congratulation', *RB* 75 (1968), p. 321-367.

origin has a special evidence in Hab. ii 6-19, where the woe-oracles are characterized with the wisdom-word *māšāl* (vs. 6); in Num. xxi 29, however, the woe-oracle to Moab (here as *'ōy lᵉkā*) is also connected with the root *mšl* (xxi 27), which does not point to a wisdom-word, but to men who recite a derision-song.

It seems to be more probable that the prophets borrowed the woe-form from the ancient mourning-cry, as CLIFFORD and WILLIAMS assumed [1]) and JANZEN recently demonstrated in his study *Mourning cry and woe oracle* [2]). This scholar has proved from examples of the ancient oriental- and greek world and of the O.T., that the three spheres in which *hōy* appears, are not so independent on each other as many scholars contended : the vocative appeal/address does not constitute a different and special type of *hōy*, but shares in a quality very characteristic of the funerary *hōy* (i.e. the sombre quality of the context) [3]), and that the latter itself shares in this appellative quality. JANZEN demonstrates further that in widespread ancient-oriental practices mourning for the dead shades over into cursing of the guilty, and : "*This shading over from sorrowful funerary lament on the one hand to invective against, yes, curse of, the guilty on the other hand embraces the whole range of content and mood in the hōy-passages*, a range which offers a genuine *Sitz im Leben* as the home of *hōy*, and which establishes an organic relationship between its apparently so diverse usages" [4]). Ugaritic evidence is to be found in the Legend of Aqhat. After the death of Aqhat, whose remains have been found in the inward of the mother of the Eagles, Dnil weeps and buries Aqhat and then curses the eagles and the place where Aqhat lived and two other places :

> Woe to thee, o Qiru-mayim (woe = *y*, also occurring as a vocative particle) on which rests the blood-guilt of Aqhat the Youth!
>
> Woe to thee, Marurat-taghullal-banir,
> on which rests the blood-guilt of Aqhat the Youth!
>
> Woe to thee, city of Abelim,
> on which rests the blood-guilt of Aqhat the Youth! [5])

---

[1]) R. J. CLIFFORD, 'The use of *hôy* in the prophets', *CBQ* 28 (1966), p. 458-464; J. G. WILLIAMS, 'The alas oracles of the 8th century prophets', *HUCA* 38 (1967), p. 75-91.

[2]) W. JANZEN, *Mourning cry and woe oracle*, BZAW 125, Berlin-New York 1972.

[3]) A possible exception is Isa. lv 1. See for details JANZEN, *o.c.*, p. 20, n. 69.

[4]) JANZEN, *o.c.*, p. 27.

[5]) ANET, p. 154 f.

Janzen invites attention for several features of this legend occurring also with Hebrew *hōy* : the curses are directed against places as in Isa. xviii 1; Nah. iii 1; Zeph. iii 1; they are found in a series as the *hōy*-oracles in Isa. v and x; they are spoken in direct address, just as the *hōy*-oracles should often be translated [1]) on account of the appellative quality that this *hōy* shares with the vocative appeal.

The same transition from mourning to revenge has been indicated by the author in Arabic and Akkadian literature (for instance in the Era Epic), in the Greek tragedies and in the O.T. : David's mourning over Saul and Jonathan, for instance, contains a curse of Mt. Gilboa (2 Sam i 21), and Isaiah's funerary lament over the faithless Jerusalem, victim of murderers, results in God's *hōy* of vengeance: Woe, I will secure a respite from my foes and take vengeance on my enemies (Isa. i 24; cf. Ez. xxiv 6-14 : Woe (here = *'ōy*) to the bloody city).

The connection between mourning-cry and prophetic woe-oracle gets still more probability by the fact that the punishment announced by the woe-oracle is often expressed "in terms which take up the very terminology or imagery of the indictment" [2]) : Woe to you, destroyer (*šōdēd*), yourself undestroyed (*lō šādūd*),... you will be destroyed (*tūšad*), (Isa. xxxiii 1; cf. Isa. v 8 f., 11-13; etc.). People that killed other people, literally or metaphorically, and thus caused mourning, are threatened by the prophetic woe to be killed themselves. Therefore Wanke can say : "Das wohl ursprünglich der Totenklage zugehörige *hōy* soll deutlich machen dass einem bestimmten menschlichen Verhalten der Keim des Todes bereits innewohnt." [3])

The demonstrated interrelatedness of the various usages of *hōy* leads for our text Am. v 18 to the following conclusion :

a. The *hōy*-word is probably not meant as an impersonal pronouncement of general truths [4]) and still less as a wisdom-proverb [5]) : 'Woe unto them that long for the Day of the Lord', but rather as the prophet's direct address to his hearers : 'Woe unto you that long for the Day of the Lord'.

b. It is probably not accidental, that Amos' *hōy*-oracles are placed in a context, which is dominated by the choice between death and

---

[1]) Janzen, *o.c.*, p. 29.

[2]) Janzen, *o.c.*, p. 35.

[3]) Wanke, *o.c.*, p. 218.

[4]) Cf. Wanke, *o.c.*, p. 217 f.

[5]) Against Gerstenberger and Wolff.

life (v 14), the accusation of people that don't seek the good but bring about misery and death for the poor (vs. 7-12; cf. vs. 14 f.), and the announcement of the Lord's verdict as His threatening visitation, that will bring death and mourning over themselves (vs. 16 f.):

> There shall be wailing in all streets,
> and in all open places they shall say: alas, alas!

The Hebrew mourning-cries, used here: *hō hō*, a variant of *hōy*, are probably meant as an audible association with the prophet's woe-oracle. The *hō hō* of the mourners (vs. 16)... seems "to be identical in motivation and content with the *hōy* of vs. 18, called out by the prophet over the secure people who will be overtaken by the darkness of the Day of the Lord... The *hōy* of vs. 18 projects a contrast to the expected Day of light and brightness (vs. 18, 20), but that contrast consists of mourning" [1]), as the association with vs. 16 f. suggests.

It is noteworthy, that the woe-oracle v 18-20 lacks the clear accusation belonging to a normal prophetic doomword. The accusation is only suggested by the participle *hammit'awwīm*, 'the people longing for the Day of the Lord', who are probably thought to be identical with those Israelites who acted in self-reliant independence of God by a behaviour 'defiant of covenant obligations towards the poor and needy' [2]) (vs. 7-15).

The announcement of the Lord's verdict is also less direct than normally; it is only evoked through the rhetorical questions of vs. 18 and 20. These questions (with their contrast between the light of the Lord's Day, as expected by the self-reliant Israelites, and the darkness of the Day announced by Amos) were probably clear enough for the audience that had heard the preceding verdict of death and mourning (vs. 15 f.).

Am. v 18-20 is the only prophecy combining the *hōy*-call and the *yōm yhwh*-motif, but there are several examples of *yōm yhwh*-prophecies in which the mourning motif, in the form of the exhortation *hēlīlū*, 'wail,' is used against Judah and Jerusalem (Joel i 5 ff.; Zeph. i 11) or against foreign peoples (Isa. xiii 6; Ez. xxx 2, with: *hāh layyōm*) in connection with the approaching Day of the Lord.

Amos was the first prophet, who left us the old mourning-cry in

---

1) Janzen, *o.c.*, p. 46.
2) Janzen, *o.c.*, p. 82.

the form of a woe-oracle, and the phrase *yōm yhwh*. The question must remain unanswered, whether Amos was also the man who coined the prophetic woe-oracle, or adopted it from others whose words have not been handed down to us. As for the phrase *yōm yhwh*, it seems to be clear that it was not coined by Amos [1]), but—as usually is acknowledged in modern exegesis—was already known as the great Day of salvation for the elected people of God, a day they ardently longed for. The question then must arise, where this phrase had its origin, where it had its 'Sitz im Leben'. The answers given to this question, are very different.

1. GRESSMANN [2]) considers the *yōm yhwh* as the beginning of Israelite eschatology, and according to him this eschatology is very old. He even speaks of pre-historic eschatology [3]). Its origin is to be found in Babylonian mythological conceptions concerning a cosmic catastrophe. These conceptions belonged to the ancient Oriental opinion that the world history can be divided into a number of successive periods, each of them ending by a destruction of the old world and followed by the creation of a new world. This theory is based upon the observation of Babylonian astronomers "that the point of the sunrise at the beginning of spring, changes a little year by year, so that it seems as if the sun in the course of hundreds and thousands of years should go right round the earth" [4]). This precession of the spring point of the sun was the basis for the theory of GRESSMANN's teacher GUNKEL : Endzeit = Urzeit [5]) : "When the sun comes back to the point where it started at the beginning, then also must be repeated every thing that has happened since the primeval age" [4]). The cosmico-mythological conceptions came into Canaan in pre-prophetic times, and existed then already as a coherent system with two contrary aspects : the woe- and the weal-eschatology. The Israelites borrowed their material from this eschatology in a fragmentary way : In the popular eschatology the *yōm yhwh* became a day in which the Lord would judge and destroy Israel's enemies, who then took the place of the mythological powers

---

1) Against M. WEISS, 'The origin of the 'Day of the Lord' reconsidered', *HUCA* 37, p. 29-60; and C. CARNITI, 'L'espressione 'Il giorno di JHWH'. Origine ed evoluzione semantica,' *Bibbia e Oriente* 12 (1970), p. 11-25.

2) H. GRESSMANN, *Der Ursprung der jüdisch-israelitischen Eschatologie*, Göttingen 1905.

3) GRESSMANN, *o.c.*, p. 147.

4) H. GUNKEL, *Genesis*, Göttingen 1901, p. 242.

5) H. GUNKEL, *Schöpfung und Chaos in Urzeit und Endzeit*, Göttingen 1895, p. 367.

of evil. Hence, Amos (followed by the other prophets) found the phrase *yōm yhwh* already as a firm formula, but he stresses the ethical demands and the fact that the Day of the Lord will be for Israel first of all a day of disaster [1]).

The theory of GUNKEL—GRESSMANN evokes several objections :

a. The idea of a cyclical world-catastrophe does not occur in the O.T.

b. Not all the *yōm yhwh*-places in the O.T. are connected with the future, let alone eschatology. In Lam. ii 22, the Day of the Lord's wrath is even spoken of as already being past with the fall of Jerusalem in 587 b. C.

c. GRESSMANN over-emphasizes the physical side of the Day of the Lord and neglects all historical references, especially the frequent references to the wrong social conditions in Israel.

d. The oldest O.T. evidences of the *yōm yhwh* don't contain any cosmo-mythological features. The first prophecy that might be interpreted from that background is the description of the Day in Zeph. i 15 [2]) as 'a day of wrath, a day of anguish and affliction, a day of destruction and devastation, a day of murk and gloom, a day of cloud and dense fog, a day of trumpet and battle-cry', but even there, as WEISS has demonstrated [3]), the clouds (cf. Ez. xxx 3) are rather an elaboration of the darkness-motif of Am. v 18, 20 than a usage of mythological material. That material occurs only in the late 'apocalyptic' descriptions of the Day of the Lord, attributed by GRESSMANN [4]) to a second incursion of the old mythological eschatology into Canaan (after the exile).

e. The most striking Babylonian parallel with the *yōm 'af yhwh*, an O.T. equivalent of the phrase *yōm yhwh* (see p. 128), occurs in the myth of Ira : *ûmu uggatika*, but this myth has no connection with the creation story or the scheme of Urzeit-Endzeit. And even from the Babylonian *ûmu uggatika* the idea of the *yōm yhwh* is not yet explained [5]).

f. By removing the problem of the origin of the *yōm yhwh* idea into

---

1) GRESSMANN, *o.c.*, p. 149-157; H. GRESSMANN, *Der Messias*, Göttingen 1929, p. 77 ff.

2) GRESSMANN, *Ursprung*, p. 144.

3) WEISS, *o.c.*, p. 49 f.

4) GRESSMANN, *o.c.*, p. 157, 247.

5) L. ČERNY, *The day of Yahweh and some relevant problems*, Prague 1948, p. 34 f.

another country, outside Israel, *unless we find a solution of it there*, we do not explain it at all [1]).

2. Another group of scholars sought the origin of the *yōm yhwh* in Israel's cult. As there where 'days of the Baalim', the Day of the Lord would originally have been a festival day in honour of Yhwh. According to MOWINCKEL [2]) this day was the first day of the great autumn-festival, New Year's day, the day of Yhwh's enthronement. From the whole of cultic ideas, connected with this festival, the prophetic *yōm yhwh*, embracing the whole picture of Israelite eschatology, would have come into existence as a projection of the yearly expectation of the cult realities into an indefinite future : "The whole picture of the future can be summed up in the expression, 'the Day of Yahweh'. Its original meaning is really the day of his manifestation or epiphany, the day of His festival and particularly that festal day which was also the day of His enthronement, His royal day, *the* festival of Yahweh, the day when as king He came and 'wrought salvation for His people'. As the people hoped for the realisation of the ideal kingship, particularly when reality fell furthest short of it, so, from a quite early period, whenever they were in distress and oppressed by misfortune, they hoped for and expected a glorious day of Yahweh..., when Yahweh must remember his covenant, and appears as the mighty king and deliverer, bringing a 'day' upon His own and His people's enemies..., condemning them to destruction, and 'acquitting' and 'executing justice' for His own people" [3]).

The following objections should be made against MOWINCKEL's theory :

a. Though he stresses (against GRESSMANN) the fact that Hebrew

---

1) ÇERNY, *o.c.*, p. 35.

2) S. MOWINCKEL, *Psalmenstudien II. Das Thronbesteigungsfest Jahwäs und der Ursprung der Eschatologie*, Kristiania 1922, and : 'Jahves dag', *Norsk T.T.* 59 (1958), p. 209-229. A cultic origin of the *yōm yhwh* is also vindicated by G. HÖLSCHER, *Die Ursprünge der jüdischen Eschatologie*, Giessen 1925, p. 12 f.; A. S. KAPELRUD, *Joel-studies*, Uppsala 1948, and : *Central ideas in Amos*, Oslo 1956; J. D. W. WATTS, *Vision and prophecy in Amos*, Rüschlikon/Zch. 1958; J. MORGENSTERN, 'Amos Studies', *HUCA* 11 (1936); 12-13 1937-'38); 15 (1940); R. LARGEMENT—H. LEMAÎTRE, 'Le jour de Yahweh...', *Sacra pagina* 1, Paris 1959, p. 259-266; R. E. CLEMENTS, *Prophecy and covenant*, London 1965, p. 107 ff.; J. LINDBLOM, *Prophecy in ancient Israel*, Oxford 1962, p. 317 ff.; K. D. SCHUNCK, 'Der 'Tag Jahwes' in der Verkündigung der Propheten', *Kairos* NF 11 (1969), p. 14-21 : originally 'ein Festtag für Jahwe'.

3) S. MOWINCKEL, *He that cometh*, Oxford 1956, p. 145.

eschatology was quite unique amongst all the ancient near-eastern nations and that its origins must be sought in the Hebrew religion only, his enthronement-festival has also a mythical, Babylonian origin, even if in Israel it became a historical background so that the elements of the enthronement could form an autochthonous cultic and ideological context.

b. The thesis that Israel celebrated a New-Year festival with the enthronement of God as most important theme (as in the Babylonian *akîtu* festival the enthronement of the king and the God Marduk), is mainly based upon the exegesis of some Psalms (xlvii, xcvi-xcix) [1]), but remains for the rest a hypothesis.

c. The main theme of the supposed enthronement-festival, the call *yhwh mālak*, does not occur in the *yōm yhwh*-texts [2]). MOWINCKEL must agree himself that all "the different singularities of the eschatological outlook are not at all ...in the express connection and organic union with the ideas of the enthronement..."; they are even "as single and only loose features juxtaposed, and their unifying point was scarcely known to the prophets" [1]).

d. If Israel indeed celebrated the enthronement-festival, the question has not yet been answered why Israel alone, from the ritual of this festival, arrived at the unique idea of an eschatological *yōm yhwh*, whereas the other nations celebrating the same festival did not so.

e. If the 'eschatological' *yōm yhwh* arose from the original cultic one on account of the yearly disappointment of the people by their God-king, how then could they trust their national God for the future [3]) ?

3. A third group of scholars, particularly G. VON RAD [4]), thought

---

1) S. MOWINCKEL, *Psalmenstudien II*, p. 230 f.

2) The motif of Yhwh's kingship occurs in Ob. 21, but this vs. can hardly be regarded as the continuation of vs. 15 ff. So it only occurs in the late text Zech. xiv 9, but even there the connection with the enthronement-festival is very doubtful, see ČERNY, *o.c.*, p. 74.

3) Cf. ČERNY, *o.c.*, p. 76.

4) G. VON RAD, 'The origin of the concept of the day of Yahweh', *JSS* 4 (1959), p. 97-108; and : *Theologie des Alten Testaments II*, München 1960, p. 133-137. Before VON RAD the *yōm yhwh*-idea was connected with God's victory in the ancient isr. wars by : J. WELLHAUSEN, *Israelitische und jüdische Geschichte*, Berlin 1914, p. 25; J. M. POWIS SMITH, 'The day of Yahweh', *AJTh* 5 (1901), p. 505 ff.; R. H. CHARLES, according to ČERNY, *o.c.*, p. 27 f. After VON RAD the connection of *yōm yhwh* and *holy war* has been stressed by K. D. SCHUNCK, 'Strukturlinien in der Entwicklung der Vorstellung vom

the origin of the *yōm yhwh* to be in the ancient Israelite institution of the 'holy war' : the starting-point of VON RAD's view is the conviction that the preaching of the prophets was based in fact on the actualization of the Israelite traditions. His study rests on the 'form- und traditionsgeschichtliche Methode' and tries to answer the question, whether the *yōm yhwh* was connected with a special 'Gattung'. It seems to be correct that VON RAD confines his inquiry to the places that mention the *yōm yhwh* expressis verbis, and leaves out of consideration those prophecies, in which the relation with the *yōm yhwh* is still problematic. On the other hand, he stresses the necessity of involving the phraseology of the context in the examination.

Though Am. v 18 is the oldest occurrence of the phrase *yōm yhwh*, VON RAD does not start his examination with that text, because Amos speaks of the Day of the Lord in a too fragmentary way, mentioning only the darkness-motif, the only one he needs in the situation of his prophecy : "It is advisable to begin with texts which convey a more unequivocal, and at the same time a broader conception of the Day of Yahweh", Isa. xiii (against Babylon), Isa. xxxiv (against Edom), Ez. vii (against the whole earth), Ez. xxx (against Egypt), Jo. ii (against Juda), which texts we must try to understand, if possible, from the closed contexts of literary units [1]). According to VON RAD all these prophecies are dominated by themes of war and battle, reminding the sacral wars of Yhwh, known from the old Israelite traditions :

> The trumpet of war has to be blown (Ez. vii 14; Jo. ii 1), and the warriors have to be sanctified (Isa. xiii 1-3; Jo. iv 9; Zeph. i 7), because they are called to assemble for battle (Isa. xiii 2; Jer. xlvi 3 f.; Jo. iv 9 ff.; Zech. xiv 2), just as the warriors of the old traditions, who had also to sanctify them-selves (Jos. iii 5; 1 Sam. xxi 5 f.). Yhwh musters the host (Isa. xiii 4) as in the story of Gideon (Jud. vii). He delivers the enemies to slaughter (Isa. xxxiv 2 *heḥerīm*) as in the old traditions. The Day brings about terror and anguish among the enemies (Isa. xiii 6-8; xxii 5; Jer. xlvi 5 f.; Jo. ii 6; cf. Ez. vii 7, 17; Zeph. i 17: Zech. xiv 13), just as in the holy-war

---

'Tag Jahwes", *VT* 14 (1964), p. 319-330 (cf. however note 30); J. JEREMIAS, *Theophanie*, Neukirchen 1965; J. R. WILCH, *Time and event*, Leiden 1969, p. 94 f.; H. W. WOLFF, *Dodekapropheton*, BK xiv 2, Neukirchen 1969, p. 38 f.; G. EGGEBRECHT, *Die frühcste Bedeutung und der Ursprung der Konzeption vom 'Tage Jahwes'*, diss. Halle 1966 : origin in the 'Krieg Jahwes', not 'heiliger Krieg'. The *yōm yhwh* is regarded as both a day of war-victory and of God's royal festival by F. M. CROSS Jr., 'The divine warrior in Israel's early cult', in : *Biblical motifs*, ed. A. ALTMANN, Cambridge 1966, p. 11-30; and R. W. KLEIN, 'The Day of the Lord', *Concordia Theol. Monthly* 39 (1968), p. 517-525.

[1]) VON RAD, *JSS* 4, p. 98 f.

traditions (Ex. xv 14-16; xxiii 27 f.; Jos. ii 9, 24; v 1; etc.). Yhwh comes in person to bring disaster (Isa. xiii 9, 11; Ez. vii 9) as in Jud. v 4. Even Yhwh's voice resounds before his army (Jo. ii 11; cf. iv 16).

There will be darkness (Am. v 18,20; Jo. ii 2; Zeph. i 15) and clouds (Ez. xxx 3; Jo. ii 2; Zeph. i 15); the celestial luminaries will even darken (Isa. xiii 10; Jo. ii 10; iii 4; iv 15; Zeph. i 15), just as darkness was a motif in the ancient wars (Ex. xiv 20; Jos. xxiv 7; cf. the clouds in Jud. v 4). The earth and the heaven will tremble (Isa. xiii 13; Jo. ii 10; iv 16), just as the earth trembled in Jud. v 4 and 1 Sam. xiv 15 (Other signs in this sphere : Isa. xxxiv 4 ;Jo. iii 3).

The slaughter will be so terrible (Isa. xiii 14 ff.; cf. Zeph. i 17), that it results in a totally desolate world (Isa. xiii 20 ff.; xxxiv 9 ff.; Jo. ii 3; cf. Zeph. i 18), a land smitten with the *ḥèrèm* (Mal. iii 24), the same word as in ancient times the sacral taking over of the spoil of Yhwh (Jos. vi 18,21; vii 17; 1 Sam. xv 3,21; etc.).

The examination leads VON RAD to two conclusions : 1) The *yōm yhwh* encompasses a pure event of war, the rise of Yhwh against his enemies, his battle and his victory. 2) The whole material is of old Israelite origin : the tradition of the holy wars of Yhwh, in which the Lord appeared personally, to annihilate his enemies [1]). Elements that might point to a cultic origin, as the description of the Day as a festival with sacrifices (Zeph. i 8; Isa. xxxiv 6; Jer. xlvi 10), are to be considered as metaphorical usages [2]), and the mythical elements (darkness,earthquake) belonged from the beginning to the holy war-tradition : the later extension corresponds simply to the graving measure of political danger [3]). The prophetic announcement of the *yōm yhwh* was a bold actualization of ancient ideas : the acts of salvation which the Lord achieved from time to time for the protection of his people. That some prophets spoke also of a battle against Israel, was an interlude in the history of the concept. The later prophets returned to the Day as salvation for Israel, as shows Zech. xiv 1 ff.[4]).

The *yōm yhwh* was not originally eschatological. Even in the prophetic texts historical events as the fall of Jerusalem are retrospectively described as a *Day of the wrath of Yhwh* (Lam. ii 22; cf. Ez. xiii 5; xxxiv 12; and Isa. xxii 5, referring to 701 b.C.), just as tradition alludes to God's intervention in ancient times with the expression 'day of Midian' (Isa. ix 3, cf. x 26; Jud. vii). It could become eschatological, if the prophet considered the events of the Day as going beyond the

---

1) VON RAD, *JSS* 4, p. 103 f.
2) VON RAD, *JSS* 4, p. 102.
3) VON RAD, *JSS* 4, p. 107.
4) VON RAD, *JSS* 4, p. 105.

ancient scheme of salvation or if the events of the Day pointed beyond the hitherto existing relation between Israel and Yhwh [1]) and extended to the universal and cosmic [2]). The most constant element in the texts is the exclamation: *qārōb yōm yhwh*, 'the Day of the Lord is at hand.' It occurs 8 times (Isa. xiii 6; Ez. xxx 3; Jo. i 15; ii 1; iv 14; Ob. 15; Zeph. i 7, 14; cf. Ez. vii 7, 12) as a firmly coined formula of tradition, where it was "the old stereotyped call with which the troops were summoned to take the field in the holy wars, or a cry with which they went to battle with Yahweh" .

Apart from the latter utterance which lacks any evidence in the ancient traditions *qārōb* saying no more than that the Day is expected to come soon [3]), VON RAD's whole theory has been thoroughly refuted by M. WEISS [4]). Here it will be enough to mention only a few objections against VON RAD :

a. Passing the question whether the institution of the holy war existed in Israel at all [5]), the war-element is far from being constitutive in the *yōm yhwh* prophecies. A third of these prophecies (among others Am. v) lack any hint of a battle. Many other prophecies, on the contrary, threaten warlike attacks by the Lord [6]) without any allusion to the *yōm yhwh*. Where then does the specific character of the Lord's Day remain?

b. Most of VON RAD's 'constituent' elements are to be found in Isa. xiii and Jo. ii, chapters which betray a clear affinity to each other [7]) and belong to the younger prophecies about the subject, in which some elements appear to be later elaborations of the sober themes in the oldest prophecies Am. v 18-20 and Isa. ii, chapters that VON RAD wrongly disregarded. So the darkness-motif of Am. v 18-20, a metaphor for general distress and disaster and not at all specific for the holy war,

---

1) VON RAD, *JSS* 4, p. 106.

2) VON RAD, *JSS* 4, p. 107.

3) KLEIN, *o.c.*, p. 521.

4) M. WEISS, 'The origin of the 'Day of the Lord', reconsidered', *HUCA* 37 (1966), p. 29-60.

5) G. FOHRER, 'Prophetie und Geschichte', *ThL* 89, col. 488; R. SMEND, *Jahwekrieg und Stämmebund*, Göttingen 1963, p. 28 f.; F. STOLZ, *Jahwes und Israels Kriege*, Zürich 1972; M. WEIPPERT, '«Heiliger Krieg» in Israel und Assyrien', *ZAW* 84 (1972), p. 460-493.

6) G. VON RAD, *Der heilige Krieg im alten Israel*, Göttingen-Zürich 1965, p. 67; J. A. SOGGIN, 'Der prophetische Gedanke über den heiligen Krieg als Gericht gegen Israel', *VT* 10 (1960), p. 81 f.

7) H. W. WOLFF, *BK* XIV 2, p. 55 f.

has been elaborated in Zeph. i 15: 'a day of murk and gloom, a day of cloud and dense fog' (cf. Ez. xxx 3; Isa. xiii 10; Jo. ii 2, 10) and has only in the late text of Jo. iii 4 become the physical darkening of the celestial bodies [1]).

c. Some of VON RAD's constitutive elements rather belong to the old theophany descriptions than in those preserved about the holy wars, particularly the motifs of Yhwh's voice (Jo. ii 11; iv 16) and of the trembling heaven and earth [2]).

d. Sacral conduct (*qdš*, Isa. xiii 2; Jo. iv 9) is not specific for the holy war; in Zeph. i 7 it is demanded in connection with a sacrificial meal as in 1 Sam. xvi 5, because God is thought to be present there. So first of all it is a theme of theophany (cf. Ex. xix 10 f.; 14) [3]).

e. Trumpet and alarm (Zeph. i 16; cf. Jo. ii 1) are neither specific for war: they serve as a sign of alarm at times of distress in general. [4])

Concluding, WEISS accentuates that the phrase *yōm yhwh* has a wider meaning and context than a pure event of war. The essential element, common to all the *yōm yhwh*-prophecies, is the theophany [5]).

4. A fourth group of scholars stress the connection between the *yōm yhwh*-idea and the covenant. FENSHAM [6]), for instance, agrees with VON RAD that some of the *yōm yhwh*-prophecies have connections with the holy war-tradition (Ez. xiii 5; Jer. xlvi 10; Zeph. i 16); he denies, however, that all the ideas can be classified under the concept of war and asks the question: If the *yōm yhwh* is to be explained from the setting of the holy war, why in the majority of cases should the destructive effect of the Day be prophesied against Israel and not, as in ancient times, against the enemies of Israel? [7]) He concludes that the Day of the Lord is not only a day of battle; it is a day of judgment and punishment; and that in a twofold sense: either for Israel's enemies

---

[1]) WEISS, *o.c.*, p. 35,51-53,58-60.

[2]) J. JEREMIAS, *Theophanie*, Neukirchen 1965, p. 99 f.; cf. J. BOURKE, 'Le Jour de Yahvé dans Joël', *RB* 66 (1959), p. 5-31, esp. p. 23-28.

[3]) WEISS, *o.c.*, p. 33 f.

[4]) WEISS, *o.c.*, p. 37.

[5]) WEISS, *o.c.*, p. 40.

[6]) F. C. FENSHAM, 'A possible origin of the concept of the Day of the Lord,' *Biblical essays of Die Outestamentiese Werkgemeenskap in Suid Afrika*, 1966, Potchefstroom 1967, p. 90-97.

[7]) FENSHAM, *o.c.*, p. 90 f.

or for Israel itself. This double character of the Day should be seen as a result of the covenant between Yhwh and Israel is the light of Near Eastern vassal-treaties. According to the clauses of these treaties the main partner promised protection against enemies, but, if a treaty or a covenant should be broken by the minor partner, the major partner might punish the breaking of the oath of the gods by a punitive expedition against the transgressor, in order to exact on him the curses which were incorporated in the treaty. The punishment for breach of contract was probably exacted either as a final stage of a lawsuit (the *rîb*-pattern) [1]) or as an ordeal by battle [2]). But battle or war was only one of many curses which might overtake a transgressor, like a severe drought, wailing in the street, darkness (cf. Am. v 16-20), etc [3]).

These treaty-curses are the real background of the Israelite concept : *yōm yhwh*. It is a day of visitation and execution of curses : the foreign enemies only receive punishment in the form of executed curses, the unfaithful Israel receives judgment as result of the breach of covenant and then punishment in the form of executed curses [4]).

Before FENSHAM similar ideas were already expressed by HÉLÉWA [5]). This author stressed the dependence of the *yōm yhwh* as directed against Israel on the lists of blessings and curses belonging to the covenant tradition of Deut. xxviii. These curses contain besides defeat in war (vs. 25) all kinds of disaster as drought, fire, locusts, disease, etc : "Les bienfaits que l'alliance est destinée à porter à un Israël fidèle se changeront en malheurs—et en malheurs opposés—au cas où Israël cessera de respecter l'engagement pris". The covenant-curses mean "un renversement complet des réalités de l'Histoire du salut, un annullement total de tout ce que Yahvé, au temps de grâce, a fait en faveur de son peuple" [6]). The *yōm yhwh* as directed against the *gōyīm* (the 'holy war',

---

1) Cf. J. HARVEY, 'Le "Rîb-Pattern" réquisitoire prophétique sur la rupture de l'alliance', *Bib.* 43 (1962), p. 172-196; H. B. HUFFMON, 'The Covenant Lawsuit in the Prophets', *JBL* 78 (1959), p. 285-295.

2) FENSHAM, *o.c.*, p. 93.

3) F. C. FENSHAM, 'Common Trends in Curses of the Near Eastern and Kudurru-Inscriptions compared with Maledictions of Amos and Isaiah', *ZAW* 75 (1963), p. 155-175; D. R. HILLERS, *Treaty Curses and the O.T. prophets*, Rome 1964; D. J. McCARTHY, 'Covenant in the O.T.', *CBQ* 27 (1965), p. 232.

4) FENSHAM, 'A possible origin', p. 95 f.

5) F. J. HÉLÉWA, 'L'origine du concept prophétique du 'Jour de Yahvé', *Ephemerides Carmeliticae* 15 (1964), p. 3-36.

6) HÉLÉWA, *o.c.*, p. 23 f.; 27.

considered as a sacral institution [1])), is also dependent on ideological categories belonging to the covenant. Disaster will fall upon the enemies on account of the injustice caused to Israel, the people of God in virtue of the covenant [2]). Theophany, belonging to the kernel of the ideological complex surrounding the *yōm yhwh*, has no less relation to the cult-tradition of the covenant of Sinai in which Yhwh appeared in order to save or to chastise his people. The connection between the *yōm yhwh* and the convenant-tradition is corroborated by the cultic colour in several contexts, e.g. the liturgies of lamentation and repentance in Joel and the representation of the Day as a sacrificial meal, prepared by Yhwh for his invited guests (Isa. xxxiv 6 f.; Zeph. i 7 f.; Jer. xlvi 10) [3]). MOWINCKEL's thesis, that the *yōm yhwh* belongs to a special festival, is seen by HÉLÉWA as an exaggeration, but he thinks too, that only the cult can explain in the *yōm yhwh*-texts the survival of the ideological, literary and imaginative elements from the traditions of covenant and holy war, which traditions are partly cultic themselves.

Though I tend to agree with HÉLÉWA and FENSHAM, that the covenant-idea is the best background for explaining the double character of the *yōm yhwh* prophecies (both against the nations and against Israel), there remain several questions that can not be answered in this way. Hence the following objections :

a) 'Covenant curses' are also used in other prophecies than those of the Day of the Lord, and so they cannot be specific for the *yōm yhwh*.

b) The difference made by FENSHAM, that the *yōm yhwh* would be for Israel a day of judgment and punishment, and for the foreign enemies only a day of punishment, is disputable; according to Jo. iv 12 f. the Lord wil 'judge the nations' in the 'valley of the Lord's judgment'.

c) (against HÉLÉWA) From the many curses of Deut. xxviii 20 ff.

---

1) Cf. G. VON RAD, *Der heilige Krieg*; R. DE VAUX, *Les institutions de l'A.T. II*, Paris 1960, p. 73-86.

2) HÉLÉWA, *o.c.*, p, 26. note 75 : "Etant donnée la relation très speciale que l'alliance biblique introduisit entre Israël et son Dieu d'une part, et la conception isr. de l'universelle seigneurerie de Yahvé, d'autre part, les malédictions contre les nations appartiennent tout aussi légitimement que les malédictions contre Israël au fond le plus authentique de la tradition de l'alliance".

3) HÉLÉWA, *o.c.*, p. 36; cf. p. 31 : The theophanies of the *yōm yhwh* belong to the cult "dans le sens d'une dépendance idéologique profonde et doivent être réferées à la tradition cultuelle du Sinaï pour la raison qu'elles représentent des applications secondaires de réalités idéologiques et cultuelles vécues dans la liturgie festive de l'alliance".

(pestilence and other diseases; drought and blight; dust instead of rain; defeat in battle; tumours, madness and blindness; oppression by cruel enemies; robbery of all kinds of possessions, wife and children included; malignant boils; deportation; locusts and grubs, etc.) only those curses, that speak of defeat and oppression by the enemy, occur in many prophecies of the *yōm yhwh* (famine and pestilence only in Ez. vii 15; locusts and drought in Joel i are only the prelude of the future Day) [1]). On the other hand, many motifs of the *yōm yhwh*-passages (e.g. darkening of the stars, clouds, earthquake) don't occur at all among the curses of Deut. xxviii, while the motif of darkness has an other meaning in Deut. xxviii 29 (after-effect of madness and blindness). So this chapter can hardly be considered as the background of our prophecies.

d) The covenant-theory does no more answer the question about the origin of the expression *yōm yhwh* than the other one's did.

Therefore we have to ask first of all what is meant by the two words *yōm yhwh* (16 x : Isa. xiii 6,9; Ez. xiii 5; Jo. i 15; ii 1,11; iii 4; iv 14; Am. v 18 (2 x), 20; Ob. 15; Zeph. i 7,14 (2x); Mal. iii 24; cf. *yōm zèbaḥ yhwh*, Zeph. i 8; *yōm ʿèbrat yhwh*, Zeph. i 18; Ez. vii 19; *yōm ʾaf yhwh*, Zeph. ii 2,3; Lam. ii 22), also occurring in the form *yōm l^{e}yhwh* (2 x : Isa. ii 12; Ez. xxx 3; cf. *yōm bāʾ l^{e}yhwh*, Zech. xiv 1; *yōm nāqām /l^{e}yhwh*, Isa. xxxiv 8; *yōm nāqām lēlōhēnū*, Isa. lxi 2; *yōm m^{e}hūmā... ladōnāy yhwh ṣ^{e}bāʾōt*, Isa. xxii 5; *w^{e}hayyōm hahū ladōnāy yhwh ṣ^{e}bāʾōt yōm n^{e}qāmā...*, Jer. xlvi 10). The latter constructions (*yōm l^{e}yhwh*, etc.) show, that *yōm* has been regarded here as indetermined [2]), and that consequently the very date of this 'Day of the Lord' was considered as unknown to the Israelites [3]). Nevertheless, the word *yōm* (occurring some 2000 times in the O.T.) points to a certain day. Pedersen and other scholars described the concept of time in the O.T. as follows : "Time is charged with substance or, rather, it is identical with its substance; time is the development of the very events... The time or day of the man or the people is therefore identical with his or its actions and fate. When mention is made of the day of Jerusalem, Jezreel or Midian, then it applies to events of decisive importance in

---

1) E. Kutsch, 'Heuschreckenplage und Tag Jahwes in Joel 1-2,' *ThZ* 18 (1962), p. 81-94. Bourke (*RB* 66, p. 12 f.; 15 f.) however identifies the plague of locusts with the *yōm yhwh* in Jo. i-ii, and considers it as the fulfilment of the curses of Deut. xxviii.

2) P. Joüon, *Grammaire de l'hébreu biblique*, Rome 1923, § 130.

3) Fensham, 'A possible origin...', p. 91.

their lives, just as the day of Yahweh is the violent actions in which Yahweh more particularly manifests himself" [1]. "The time of the action, which for us is the principal thing, is of no importance to the Hebrews" [2]. The studies of Barr and Wilch [3], however, have demonstrated that this thesis needs some modifications : There should be made difference between *'ēt*, 'time', and *yōm*, 'day'. "The word *'ēt* is used in the O.T. in order to indicate the relationship or juncture of circumstances, primarily in an objective sense and only secondarily in a temporal sense, and to direct attention to a specifically definite occasion or situation" [4]. In distinction to *'ēt*, that refers directly to the occasion itself, the singular *yōm* is ordinarily employed purely for *temporal references*, retaining the basic meaning *day*, which indicates both the *temporality* of the occasion and its localization at a certain time. As in our usage of the word 'day', *yōm* either indicates the space of time marked by the light of the sun, as contrasted with *laylā*, 'night' (Gen. i 14; cf. xviii 1; Jud. xix 8 f., 11; etc.), or the space of time from one evening till the next one (Gen. i 5,8, etc.). Nevertheless, "*yōm* may also imply a qualitative aspect of the particular occasion as...: 'the day of evil' (Am. vi 3)", or "refer to *crisis* situations", e.g. 'on the day of battle' (Am. i 14); 'on the day of punishment' (Isa. x 3), and particularly in the expression *yōm yhwh*. However, the Day of the Lord "is not in itself a substance that is 'filled', but is only the *means* of referring to the intervening activity of God" [5]. In which way then does the expression *yōm yhwh* refer to God's intervention? Wilch recurs, with Von Rad and many other scholars, to expressions like *yōm yizr^{e}'èl*, *yōm midyān*, *yōm miṣrayim*, *yōm y^{e}rūšālayim* (respectively Hos. ii 2; Isa. ix 3; Ez. xxx 9; Ps. cxxxvii 7), which refer all to a certain day of battle. Hence *yōm yhwh* would indicate the 'Day of the Lord's battle', or briefly "the Battle of Yhwh' [6]. Apart from the fact that several *yōm yhwh*-passages (e.g. Am. v 18-20) don't contain the slightest allusion to a

---

1) J. Pedersen, *Israel, its life and culture I-II*, London-Copenhagen 1926, p. 487 f.

2) Cf. Weiss, *o.c.*, p. 46; S. Herrmann (*Heilserwartungen im A.T.*, Stuttgart 1965, p. 121) : "Der Begriff 'Tag' umschreibt den Ereignis- und Geschehnischarakter eines machtvollen Geschehens und seine Wirkungen".

3) J. R. Wilch, *Time and event*, Leiden 1969; J. Barr, *Biblical words for time*, London 1969², p. 106 f.

4) Wilch, *o.c.*, p. 164; cf. p. 21 ff.

5) Wilch, *o.c.*, p. 166; cf. p. 47, 52-59, 62-64, 67-72; 89-102, particulary p. 92-95; cf. Carniti, *o.c.*, p. 12-14.

6) Wilch, *o.c.*, p. 95.

battle [1]), the expressions are not fully comparable either, because *yōm* in the expressions of battle has a geographical name as nomen rectum, while in *yōm yhwh* the nomen rectum is a personal name. In that respect the phrases *y^e^mē habb^e^ʿālīm*, 'the (holy) days of the baalim' and *yōm ḥag yhwh* (Hos. ii 15; ix 5; cf. Acc. *ûmu ili*) might offer a better parallel, but we had already to refute the thesis of MOWINCKEL, considering the original *yōm yhwh* as a special festival day [2]).

In relation to our subject, ČERNY [3]) called attention to the words that David spoke, when he refused to put an end to Saul: "...the Lord will strike him down; either his day, *yōmō*, will come and he will die, or he will go down to battle and meet his end". A man's *yōm* is the day of his final destiny, on which the Lord will strike him down (1 Sam. xxvi 10; cf. Jer. l 27; Ez. xxi 30; Ob. 12; Ps. xxxvii 13; Job. xviii 20). In the phrase *yōm yhwh*, the Lord can not be, of course, the object of that final destiny. Nowhere in the O.T. Yhwh is considered as a dying God like Baal; on the contrary, He is the living God [4]). Therefore, Yhwh has to be considered as the subject, the One who decrees and brings about the final destiny, the death of men, just like in the words of David.

ČERNY points out, that this conception of the *yōm yhwh* is very near to the 'dangerous days', the *ûmē uḫulgallê* or *ûmê limnûti* of Assyro-Babylonian hemerologies, and that one of the Assyrian *uḫulgallê* days, the ninth day of the month, was called in Ashur 'the (day) of the wrath of Gula', comparable with the Hebrew phrase *yōm 'af yhwh* (Zeph. ii 2,3; Lam. ii 22). Yet, the author must agree that the Day of the Lord can not be identified with an *ûmu limnu* : "The danger in an *ûmu limnu* is transcendent above the limits of human power, but if the prescribed proper way is scrupulously followed, the danger may be avoided. The danger hidden in the Day of Yahweh falls upon men as a consequence of their 'wrong ways' and as 'decreed' by Yahweh when his 'long suffering' has been exhausted it cannot be avoided. Only if men change their 'ways' and then, only those who truly change them, may be spared by Yahweh's grace, but the 'decreed' course of things cannot be averted" [5]). Whatever may be the connection with

---

1) See p. 124.

2) See p. 120 f.; cf. for the Day as a cultic day : E. F. WEIDNER, 'Der Tag des Stadtgottes', *AfO* 14 (1941-'44), p. 340-342.

3) ČERNY, *o.c.*, p. 77.

4) Cf. e.g. A. R. HULST, *Confrontatie met de levende God*, dies-rede Utrecht 1967.

5) ČERNY, *o.c.*, p. 79.

the Mesopotamian 'dangerous days', the Day of the Lord can best be conceived as the day of disaster and death decreed and brought about by Yhwh. All the features of the descriptions of the Day fit in with this conception, and consequently all the positive elements of the recent studies on the subject can be reduced to this denominator : *yōm yhwh* is a day of theophany on which the Lord appears [1]) (sometimes accompanied with signs in the natural spheres and with terrible effects) in order to execute the dark fate that he decreed. It is at the same time a day on which He acts as the God of the covenant with Israel, punishing with disaster and death the enemies that threatened or oppressed his people, and so were his own enemies [2]), or punishing his own people Israel, when it had unfaithfully broken the covenant (cf. p. 125 f.). The Day of the Lord could be a day of battle (cf. p. 123), but war was not the only means by which God could execute his punishment. Just as Yhwh punished in ancient times the enemies of Israel in different ways (e.g. the ten Egyptian plagues in Exodus alongside of the battles of deliverance in the books Joshua and Judges), and the unfaithful Israelites were struck down by the wrath of Yhwh on the 'day of the plague' consequent on the lewd worship of Baal Peor (Num. xxv 1-5,18, not mentioning the kind of the plague) and by earthquake, fire and a 'plague' after Korah's revolt (Num. xvi f.; cf. the choice between famine, war and pestilence after David's census, 2 Sam. xxiv), so the destruction and death, as expected from the Lord's intervention on his Day, could be caused by different means, though the war-like descriptions seem to be dominant. The cult of Israel must have played a part in the development of the descriptions of the *yōm yhwh* in so far as the material of the descriptions which originated from the ancient traditions, as well as the threat of judgment, were there handed down [3]).

In our passage, Am. v 18-20, the oldest instance of the expression *yōm yhwh* in the O.T., the conception of this Day as a day of disaster and death is in complete harmony with the prophetic *hōy* derived

---

[1]) See p. 125; cf. P. VERHOEF, *Die Dag van die Here*, Den Haag 1956, p. 89 ff: " 'n dag... waarin Hy Hom beslissend en bepalend openbaar".

[2]) Cf. in a Hethite vassal-treaty: 'Wie er dir Feind (ist), ebenso er auch der Sonne Feind. Wie er der Sonne Feind (ist), so soll er dir Feind sein', translation from J. FRIEDRICH, *Die Staatsverträge des Hatti-Reiches in hethitischer Sprache*, Leipzig 1930, p. 58 f., 66 f.

[3]) Cf. HÉLÉWA, *o.c.*, p. 16; CLEMENTS, *o.c.*, p. 110.

from the mourning-cry, and with the preceding announcement of doom which is entirely dominated by expressions of death and mourning consequent on a theophany : 'for I will pass through the midst of you' (vs. 17 ; cf. *'ābar* as an expression for theophany in Ex. xxxiii 18 ff.). The ideas of death and disaster are also evoked by the image of darkness [1]) (*ḥōšèk* and *'āfēl*, vs. 18,20), while vs. 19 stresses the inescapable gravity of the coming Day. It will be as when a man, hardly escaped from death by a lion and a bear, is mortally bitten by a snake, when he has finally reached his house and thinks to be safe. Yet, Amos does probably not exclude the possibility of salvation for a remnant of faithful Israelites, the 'remnant of Joseph' (vs. 15; cf. Zeph. iii 3). Amos' *yōm yhwh*-prophecy is best understandable as a reaction of the prophet upon objections of his audience [2]) against his precedent announcement of Yhwh's passing through the midst of them (*'è'ebōr bèqirbekā*), bringing about death and mourning. Appealing to the ancient tradition of Yhwh's 'passing through the land of Egypt' (*we'ābarti be*, Ex. xii 12) they may have objected, that the day of God's intervention causing death and mourning was to be expected in another way than Amos had announced. In their self-satisfied religion, supported by the prosperity and political security under Jeroboam's government, they could only expect it as a day of God's intervention in their favour. In virtue of Yhwh's election of Israel (iii 2), they thought him to be obliged to guard their interest, and to protect them against the threatening of their enemies. They believed Yhwh to be with them in all circumstances (v 14) and so they felt secure (vi 1), thinking : 'disaster will not come near us or overtake us' (ix 10), and eliminated from their religion the other side of their particular relation with Yhwh : their special responsability. It is this side Amos had to emphasize, shocking the false feelings of security of his audience. For the very reason that Yhwh 'knew' Israel alone, he would punish them for their iniquities (iii 2). They had to experience that the Lord who delivered his people and protected them against foreign people (ii 9 ff.), the Lord who—with the approval of Israel—directed his destructive curses against the foreign nations (i 2 ff.), was at the same time the Holy One, who would intervene in his own people for the sake

---

1) Though 'darkness' may be an indication of theophany (Deut. iv 11; v 22; 2 Sam. xxii 10; Ps. xcvii 2; Job xxii 13 f.; cf. KLEIN, *o.c.*, p. 518; BOURKE, *o.c.*, p. 23 f.) it is here, as contrasted with 'light', rather metaphorically meant.

2) Cf. W. RUDOLPH, *Joel-Amos-Obadja-Jona*, KAT xiii 2, Gütersloh 1972, p. 202.

of justice, punishing them with destruction for their unfaithful behaviour towards the Lord of the covenant and the feeble members of his people : the poor and the needy (ii 6 ff.).

In v 18-20 Amos probably reacts in the same way upon complacent conceptions concerning the expected Day of the Lord, the future day of death and disaster, which they longed for, convinced as they were that the Day would bring disaster for their enemies, and consequently happiness for themselves, This expectation may have been furthered by the fact that the *yōm yhwh*-curses till then had only been pronounced against individual foreign nations, just like the curses of Am. i-ii, where, however, the phrase *yōm yhwh* does not occur (but cf. Isa. xiii, against Babylon; xxxiv, against Edom; Ez. xxx, against Egypt) [1]).

Amos and the other prophets before the exile react with the announcement, that it will also be a day of punishment for Israels iniquity and proud self-reliance (Am. v; Isa. ii; Zeph. i; Ez. vii; cf. Isa. xxii; Ez. xiii 5; Lam. ii 22). During the exile and in the first stage of restoration, when the penalty is paid, there is room again for the *yōm yhwh* as a day of punishment for Israel's enemies and salvation for Israel (Isa. xiii; xxxiv; lxi 2; Jer. xlvi; Ez. xxx; Ob.), and in the last stage of development it was interpreted as a day of universal judgment (Jo. iv; Zech. xiv). Alongside with the real new that the Lord would bring about for the remnant of Israel, we then see also an increasing attention in *yōm yhwh*-passages "to radical changes in cosmos... an emphasis that reaches full fruition in the apocalyptic tradition" (e.g. Zech. xiv) [2]).

Finally, a few words about the question whether Amos' *yōm yhwh*-prophecy can be considered as an eschatological word. We saw already that *yōm yhwh* is not in itself an eschatological phrase. It may refer to past as well as to future events [3]). But can the whole prophecy be called eschatological? If we take eschatological in the narrow sense

---

1) According to H. P. Müller (*Ursprünge und Strukturen alttestamentlicher Eschatologie*, Berlin 1969), the *yōm yhwh*-announcement belongs to the announcements of disaster against individual foreign nations, which "als solche schon in den alten Heiligen Kriegen selber laut wurde" (p. 76).

2) Klein, *o.c.*, p. 524; cf. F. Couturier, 'Le Jour de Yahvé dans l'Ancien Testament', *Revue de l'Université d'Ottawa* 24 (1954), p. 193-217; esp. p. 205 ff.; Bourke, *o.c.*, p. 18-21, 24 f.; Schunck, *VT* 14 (1964), p. 319-330, and : *Kairos* NF 11 (1969), p. 14-21. J. G. Trapiello, 'La noción del 'Día de Yahve' en el Antiguo Testamento', *Cu Bí* 26 (1969), p. 331-336.

3) See p. 123.

of the word, as referring to the end of world and history, and the beginning of a competely new one [1]), we cannot speak of eschatology before the exile. If we may take it in a broader sense, as relating to "the end of the present worldorder and the breaking in of a new divinely created order, even though the events were to take place within history and not beyond it" [2]), then the pre-exilic prophets did have an eschatology of doom [3]), and expected an intervention of God in order to bring about an absolutely new order. In that sense our text belongs to the eschatological preaching of the prophets [4]).

[1]) G. Hölscher, *o.c.*, p. 3; S. Mowinckel, *He that cometh.* p. 133 ff.; G. Fohrer, 'Die Struktur der alttestam. Eschatologie', *TLZ* 85 (1960), col. 401 ff; C. F. Whitley, *The prophetic achievement*, Leiden 1963, p. 202 ff.

[2]) Clements, *o.c.*, p. 114.

[3]) Clements, *o.c.*, p. 103 ff.

[4]) Klein, *o.c.*, p. 523; Rudolph, *o.c.*, p. 204.

THE SONS OF GOD AND THE DAUGHTERS OF MEN: GENESIS VI 2 IN EARLY CHRISTIAN EXEGESIS.

BY

L. R. WICKHAM

Southampton

Soon after 431, the year of the Council of Ephesus, when Cyril of Alexandria had emerged as victor in his contest with Nestorius of Constantinople, a letter reached him from some monks in Palestine [1]). It was the first of two addressed to him by a certain deacon Tiberius and his fellow monks and it asks for authoritative anwers on a variety of disputed points. The need for such answers, says Tiberius, has arisen out of controversies amongst the brethren. The brethren are being disturbed by intruders "attempting to sow the tares of their teachings amongst our pure wheat of piety". The species of tare need not be defined here [2]). It will be enough to say that the fifteen questions to which Cyril replied with characteristic decisiveness and uncharacteristic brevity mostly, but not exclusively, concern the conditions of the incarnation and the capacities of the incarnate Son. The last answer of Cyril provides my starting-point [3]). Headed "To those who say 'how did the demons, being incorporeal, have intercourse with women?' " the answer runs as follows : Since they say that certain people are asking how evil demons, being incorporeal, have had intercourse with women and [how] these [women] could have born (*ἐγέννων*) the giants to them, we must speak cursorily on this point too, not equalling the narrative in extent but explaining in a nutshell the meaning of the thing. Well, they say that in very early periods or times a division was made, a division, I mean between the descendants of Cain and those of Enosh who, because of his very great righteousness was called "God" by his contemporaries—"he hoped", it says, "to be called by the name

---

1) *Responsiones ad Tiberium Diaconum Sociosque* ed. PUSEY, in : *Sancti patris nostri Cyrillt... in D. Joannis evangelium. Accedunt fragmenta varia necuon tractatus ad Tiberium diaconum duo*, III, Oxford 1872, pp. 557-602.

2) It is perhaps 'Messalian'.

3) ed. PUSEY, *ibid.* pp. 600 ff.

of the Lord his God"[Genesis iv 26]. But Enosh's descendants were guardians of righteousness and of all well-doing, following the ways of their father, whereas Cain's were arrogant and accursed, ready to practise every species of wickedness, for such was the father they had. To be sure, so long as the races were unmixed with each other, the preëminence in excellence of life was maintained by Enosh's descendants. But when "the sons", it says, "of" him who was called "God" i.e. Enosh, saw Cain's daughters whom Scripture has also called "daughters of men" [Genesis vi 2], they were defiled by contact with them, became subject to foul lusts and were perverted to their ways. For this reason God was angered and caused the wives chosen by them to bear monsters, whom they also called 'giants' from the ugliness and cruelty of their ways and their savage ferocity. Moreover, the four translators who came after the Seventy, when they rendered the passage, have not written "the sons of God seeing the daughters of men" but one has "the sons of those in power" (*τῶν δυναστευόντων*) and one, "the sons of the chiefs" (*τῶν δυναστῶν*). The thought that incorporeal demons can produce the effects of bodies and accomplish what is beyond their proper nature is witless. For no entity can do what is beyond nature but each abides as it has been created, God having prescribed to each its station—he is the creator of all and by his commands each entity is what it is. This additional point is to be noted : some of the copies have "the *angels* of God seeing the daughters of men". But it is an interpolation put there from outside; the true (text) is "the *sons* of God seeing the daughters of men".

Cyril's exegesis of the passage here is substantially the same as the one he had given, perhaps a decade earlier, in his fancifully titled commentary on passages in the Pentateuch, the *Glaphyra* ("polished pieces") [1]). He was to repeat it in the *Contra Julianum*, a massive counter-blast to the apostate Emperor's *Adversus Galilaeos*, completed probably towards the end of the 430's [2]). A few differences, though, are worth a word of comment. By the time Cyril answered Tiberius

1) PG 69, 13-677.

2) PG 76, 504-1057. This work, and likewise the letter to Acacius *On the scapegoat* [= Ep. 9], were sent to John of Antioch for showing *τοῖς κατὰ τὴν Ἑῴαν διαπρέπουσι διδασκάλοις*- see Theodoret *Ep. 84* [A.C.O.2.1.2 p. 51]. Such a lengthy work can hardly have been written whilst Cyril was engaged in the Nestorian controversy between 429 and 433. The completion of the work, therefore, dates between 433 and 441 (the death of John of Antioch).

he had persuaded himself that *ἄγγελοι* was an interpolation in the text of the Septuagint. That idea had apparently not occurred to him when he wrote *Glaphyra* ii [1]). He is aware, he says, that certain copies read *ἄγγελοι* and some people interpret the passage in a thoroughly perverse and absurd manner of fallen angels. The absurdity lies in the fact that since desires follow innate impulses spirits cannot desire what is corporeal and even if *per impossible* they could, human reproduction cannot result from discarnate spirits. Some, Cyril goes on, attempt to palliate the absurdity by the suggestion that evil demons entered men and *δι' αὐτῶν εἰργάζετο τὰς τῶν σπερμάτων καταβολάς*. The notion is thoroughly coarse and ignorant. Why should we accept and count as a truth something that the holy Scripture has not said? We shall, then, take the reading *υἱοὶ τοῦ θεοῦ* support for which is given by Aquila's *υἱοὶ τῶν θεῶν* and Symmachus' *υἱοὶ τῶν δυναστευόντων*. Both designations suit the descendants of Seth and Enosh. As for the giants, they are not the fabulous beings of Greek mythology one of whom is supposed to have tossed the whole of Sicily into the sky, but ugly, savage men of unusual size but not so tall that they touched the clouds. In *Contra Julianun* ix [2]) the argument takes a slightly different turn. Julian read *υἱοὶ τοῦ θεοῦ* in his text of Genesis vi 2 but applied it to the angels. This is no metaphorical designation, Julian says, it must mean 'angels' because the offspring are giants not men. Moses knows nothing of any Only-begotten Word or Son of God. What he does know is a single, unique God with a plurality of sons or angels amongst whom the nations are distributed. To which Cyril replies that Julian's interpretation is quite beside the mark. Men are certainly called 'gods' and 'sons of the most High' (quoting Psalm lxxxi (lxxxii) 6) and how could Moses who wrote of the manifestation of God to Jacob at the river Jabbok have been ignorant of the incarnation of the Only-begotten? Julian's exegesis of Genesis vi 2 impugns the angels and is sure to encourage immorality. "Is it not probable that many will be discouraged by this and choose sensuality, despising higher things and thinking that habitual resistance to the impulses of the flesh will be quite utterably intolerable and hard for them, if we believe that even the very angels fell subject to passion?" We can easily prove that Julian has got the passage wrong. Moses wrote "sons of God" and

---

1) PG 69, 49 ff.

2) PG 76, 945 ff. For further discussion of the passage see Alexander KERRIGAN, *St. Cyril of Alexandria interpreter of the Old Testament* (Rome 1952), pp. 289 f.

Julian himself has asserted (where, Cyril does not say—it is not in the quotation from Julian) that "angels of God" is an addition to the text, whereas the better reading is "sons of God". The other translators after the Septuagint have *υἱοὶ τῶν δυναστευόντων* (neither in the *Glaphyra* nor here does he mention *τῶν δυναστῶν* and he keeps quiet, for very obvious reasons, about Aquila's *τῶν θεῶν*) and the Enosh explanation with a note on 'giants' follows.

This interpretation of Cyril's is no novelty. Innovation and the indulgence of individual imagination are not gifts or habits on which he looked favourably, at least in their application to religious truth. In matters of religious truth there is, for Cyril, a right and a wrong and wrongness and newness (one could add moral perverseness and culpable stupidity for good measure) are practically interchangeable predicates. The unyielding conservatism of Cyril must be taken into account when we evaluate his statement that *ἄγγελοι* is an interpolation; an interpolation is a novelty. But the question of the true reading of the LXX and the correct translation of בני האלהים is only one element in Cyril's exposition. The other elements may be summarised as follows: the interpretation of the phrase "sons of God" as peculiarly righteous human beings, descendants of Enosh; the impossibility of demonic lust and its consummation. Two further details must be noted. They explain the second and third elements in Cyril's exposition. First, *ἐπικαλεῖσθαι* in Genesis iv 26 [Hebrew לקרא] is taken in the passive and not the middle; secondly, interpretations based on the book of Enoch or Philo are implicitly rejected.

This second observation I can in part clarify by reference to Augustine's *De Civitate Dei* XV, 17 ff., a work written between 413 and 426 and so roughly of the same period as Cyril's *Glaphyra*. Augustine offers the explanation which in general outline was to become dominant in Western Christian exegesis until the 19th century and perhaps still has representatives amongst Christians today [1]). It differs subtly from Cyril's. Adam, according to Augustine, is the father of two lines, those who descend from Seth and belong to the heavenly city and those who descend from Cain and belong to the earthly city. To Seth, whose name means 'resurrection' was born Enosh, meaning 'man', who symbolises and prefigures the divine society as is shown by what the

---

[1]) With Jewish exegesis of the passage, reflected in the renderings *δυναστευόντων* and *δυναστῶν* I am not competent to deal.

Bible further says of him : *hic speravit invocare nomen Domini Dei.* 'Man' who is the son of 'Resurrection' hoped to call on the name of the Lord God. What clearer indication could there be of the gospel message to come? Cain, on the other hand, means 'possession'. The city he founded and the line descended from him is the community of the earth-born. It was the intermingling of these cities which produced the wickedness God punished with the Flood, a wickedness which owed its origin yet again to the female sex. The angels of God (the Sethites) saw the beauty of the daughters of men (the Cainites) and were seduced by it, abandoning a higher for a lower good. Some people think that the designation 'angels of God' is meant literally. What then of their unions with mortal women? There is nothing impossible in the idea. Angels in the Bible have palpable bodies and there are besides plenty of well-attested stories of Silvani and Pans, commonly called *incubi*, lusting after women and having intercourse with them. *Et quosdam daemones, quos Dusios Galli nuncupant, adsidue hanc inmunditiam et temptare et efficere, plures talesque adseverant, ut hoc negare impudentiae videatur.* But despite the wealth of evidence Augustine cannot believe that the angels fell at this time. Men are, after all, called 'angels' in the Bible—the prophet Malachi, for example [Malachi ii 7]. The "angels of God" in Genesis vi 2 are the "sons of God" in verse 4. As for the "giants" these are abnormally large men who existed before and after the marriages of the sons of God and women. Not all the offspring of these *mésalliances* were giants but the proportion of giants in the population was considerably greater before the Flood than after. Their existence is a lesson to the wise not to attach importance to physical beauty or size. The LXX, Augustine observes, certainly uses both titles 'angels of God' and 'sons of God' [verses 2 and 4]; not all the texts have 'angels of God', though, for some give only 'sons of God'. Aquila has "sons of gods", which coheres perfectly well with the explanation he has given. The Septuagint translators had the spirit of prophecy, so that if they changed anything by his authority and said anything different from what they were translating, it should not be doubted that this was by divine appointment [1]). As for the book of Enoch, which contains stories about giants

[1]) For Augustine's attitude towards the LXX, see *The Cambridge History of the Bible* I, Cambridge 1970, cc. 16 f. and esp. pp. 521 and 545. The undertones in his correspondence with Jerome are finely brought out by Peter BROWN's *Augustine of Hippo*, London 1967, pp. 274 f.

without human fathers, it has been rejected by responsible judges and is of doubtful antiquity and authenticity.

What were these stories in the book of Enoch explicitly rejected here by Augustine and implicitly by Cyril? The book of Enoch weaves an elaborate fantasy round Genesis vi 2 ff. "And it came to pass when the children of men had multiplied that in those days were born unto them beautiful and comely daughters. And the angels, the children of the heaven, saw and lusted after them, and said to one another: 'Come, let us choose us wives from among the children of men and beget us children' " [Enoch vi 1 f.] [1]). Fearful of the consequences of detection and unwilling to bear them alone, Semjaza, leader of the angels, demands that an oath be taken. Two hundred angels descend and take the oath on Mount Hermon. Wives are chosen to whom they teach magic and enchantments. The wives become pregnant and bear giants 3000 ells in height who consume all the acquisitions of men. The use of cosmetics and of jewelry, the techniques of dyeing clothes and other arts, darker and more questionable, are divulged to men by angels, and the human race is set fair for perdition. Variations on this fantasy are to be found elsewhere in the Apocryphal literature. Allusions to it have plausibly been found in the New Testament, especially in 2 Peter ii 4 and Jude 6—only allusions, otherwise the interpretations of Cyril and Augustine would have been impossible. Its influence is to be perceived in Philo, Josephus, Greek Christian writers up to the 3rd century and Latin writers as late as Ambrose.

The principal ingredients, then, in the interpretation of Genesis vi 2 offered by Cyril and Augustine are now before us. I propose that we turn to investigate the way in which these ingredients were, so to say, transmitted to them. It will be convenient to attend to two questions

---

[1]) R. H. CHARLES, *Apocrypha and Pseudepigrapha of the Old Testament*, II *Pseudepigrapha*, p. 191 (Oxford 1913). This article is much indebted to CHARLES' annotation of this verse. To the list of parallel passages may now be added the *Genesis Apocryphon* (col. 11).

Professor H. F. D. SPARKS reminded me at the meeting at which this paper was read of the importance of this passage in Enoch (and of Gen. vi 2 which underlies it) for the development of early Christian ideas about angelic apostasy as the cause of present ills as shown by N. P. WILLIAMS in *The Ideas of the Fall and of Original Sin* (London 1927). The naturalistic explanations of Cyril and Augustine may be seen as at least in part a rejection of any 'historical' connexion between the events of Gen. vi 2 and the original angelic fall—though indeed this happened by the time of Origen (in contrast with Justin and Athenagoras who make that connexion *vide infra*).

as we look at writers before Cyril and Augustine : first, what did the writer read in his text—'angels' or 'sons'?; secondly, how does he apply the designation—is it to super-terrestrial or earthly beings? My aim is to explain, if I can, how these interpretations of Cyril and Augustine, so different from what is generally offered by the modern exegete, established themselves. There is good reason for being particular as to the reading an early Christian writer had in his Bible text, not so much for the sake of the study of the LXX (I note that BROOKE and McLEAN print ἄγγελοι in the text with υἱοί in the notes whereas RAHLFS does the reverse) as for a reason which is not obvious to the Hebraist. Chrysostom in *Homily XXII in Genesim* [1]) rejects the interpretation 'angels' for υἱοὶ τοῦ θεοῦ. Exponents of this interpretation must first show, he says, where angels are called "sons of God" in the Bible. The Hebraist will point to Job i 6; ii 1 and xxxviii 7. The LXX, at least as given in RAHLFS, has ἄγγελοι at all three places; in Psalms xxviii (xxix) 1 and lxxxviii (lxxxix) 7, where υἱοὶ τοῦ θεοῦ translates בני אלים the reference to superhuman beings could be doubted. The application of Genesis vi 2 to human beings, can, so to say, become airborne if and when (and it may be added, only if and when) υἱοί is established as the normative reading of the text, at least so far as non-Hebraist exegetes are concerned; and that means all, or almost all, Eastern exegetes. Augustine knew no Hebrew and not much Greek; but he had probably read Jerome's notes on the passage. To these I shall briefly revert later.

I begin from Philo. In his Greek text of Genesis vi 2 he read ἄγγελοι as we can see from *De Gigantibus* c.2 [2]). Does he apply it to super-terrestrial or to earthly beings? To both, for the interpretation he offers in the place mentioned and in the subsequent chapters is, to put it summarily, allegorical and platonizing. 'Angels', what the philosphers call 'demons' and 'souls' are all of a kind; all indeed are souls. Some souls have retained their discarnate existence, disdaining contact with things corporeal, and minister to the will of the creator in special service. Other souls have descended into bodies. Not all souls are good and some evil 'angels' court the pleasures, the "daughters" (for passions are feminine and evil) born

---

[1]) PG 53, 187.

[2]) *Opera* II, pp. 42-55, ed. L. COHN and P. WENDLAND (Berlin 1896 ff.). He also read ἄγγελοι in v. 4 (see *Quod Deus sit immutabilis*, *ibid.*, p. 56) explaining it as meaning evil spirits associating with passions and producing vices.

of men. The evil angels make choice amongst the myriad daughters of men available to them. Some choose visual, others aural, gastronomic or sexual pleasures. Amongst these the Spirit of God cannot dwell, for carnality opposes what is spiritual. The giants of v. 4 are the earth-born who indulge in sensual pleasure; with these are contrasted the heaven-born (intellectual, speculative souls) and the God-born (priests and prophets, enrolled as citizens in the state of incorruptible and incorporeal ideas). According, then, to this interpretation of Philo (if I have understood it aright) Genesis vi 2 refers to the descent of certain souls into human bodies. That human bodies and immaterial spirits should intermingle is, for Philo, not an unnatural controversion of divine ordinances; human beings simply *are* earthly flesh and immaterial, pre-existent spirit. In another passage, *Questions and Answers on Genesis* I, 92 [1]). Philo gives an interpretation of 'giants' rather different from this, though perhaps not inconsistent with it. The 'giants' are a mixture of angels and mortal women. The substance of angels is spiritual, but they can imitate the forms of men and have carnal knowledge of women to produce men of extraordinary physical powers. "Sometimes he calls the angels 'sons of God' because they are... spirits without body. But rather does that exhorter, Moses, give to good and excellent men the name of 'sons of God', while wicked and evil men (he calls) 'bodies'." In this passage, be it noted, Philo admits a use of the phrase "sons of God" in application to virtuous human beings. I propose to call it his third interpretation, though again without prejudice to its consistency with the other two.

What future was the first of these interpretations to have amongst Christians? Origen clearly knew the *De Gigantibus*. He believed in pre-existent souls, he thought that every conception was an incarnation and that incarnation was descent. He alludes in *Contra Celsum* V, 55 [2]) to the view that Genesis vi 2, "the sons of God saw that the daughters of men were fair, and took to themselves wives of all whom they chose"—the view of "one of our predecessors"— refers to souls afflicted with a desire for life in a human body, but neither accepts nor rejects it. In his *Commentary on John* vi 42(25) [3]) he refers to the name Jordan with its meaning of "descent", a name linked etymologically with "Jared" son of Mahalalel in whose days, if the book of Enoch is accep-

---

1) trans. R. Marcus, *Philo Supplement I*, Loeb edition (London New York 1953).

2) Origenes II, pp. 58 f. [GCS].

3) Origenes IV, p. 151 [GCS].

ted as holy, the descent of the sons of God to the daughters of men occurred: *ἥντινα κατάβασιν αἰνίσσεσθαί τινες ὑπειλήφασι τὴν τῶν ψυχῶν κάθοδον ἐπὶ τὰ σώματα, θυγατέρας ἀνθρώπων τροπικώτερον τὸ γήϊνον σκῆνος λέγεσθαι ὑπειληφότες*. The language implies that it is not a view he himself espoused. Neither did the faithful Origenist, Didymus [1]). Unlike his master, Didymus read *ἄγγελοι τοῦ θεοῦ* in Genesis vi 2 and found himself in insuperable difficulties. Does the passage mean literally the intercourse of angels with women or has it some other meaning? Some think of sensual demons in love with bodies uniting themselves with women—but the resulting pregnancy and human reproduction excludes this. Others allegorise the passage, interpreting it of a desire by angels for bodily perception (the 'wives' with whom they are united) resulting in the birth of 'giants' ('reasonings and actions') which are bodies; God's plan is that when this desire was satiated the angels would return to their former state. Others again think of demons enjoying a vicarious satisfaction through the sin of wicked men. Didymus states the possibilities without, it seems, committing himself to any one of them. Neither Origen nor Didymus used Genesis vi 2 in any proof for the pre-existence and descent of souls. It was, we may conclude, too tricky, too uncertain for this purpose.

What of Philo's second interpretation, more closely linked with the book of Enoch and paralleled in part by Josephus *Antiquities* I, 73 [2])? Justin (*Second Apology* 5) [3]), Irenaeus (*Adversus Haereses* IV, 36,4 [4]); *Demonstration* 18) [5]), Athenagoras (*Legatio* 24, 5 f) [6]), Clement of Alexandria (*Stromata* V,1) [7]), Ps-Clementine *Homily* VII, 12-15 [8]) all

---

1) Prof. P. Nautin generously transcribed for me the relevant passage from the Tura-papyrus *Commentary on Genesis*—the edition of which he has undertaken.

2) ed. H. St. J. Thackeray, Loeb edition (London New York 1930). Josephus calls them 'angels' but does not cite the text : *πολλοὶ γὰρ ἄγγελοι θεοῦ γυναιξὶ συνίοντες ὑβριστὰς ἐγέννησαν παῖδας καὶ παντὸς ὑπερόπτας καλοῦ διὰ τὴν ἐπὶ τῇ δυνάμει πεποίθησιν. ὅμοια γὰρ τοῖς ὑπὸ γιγάντων τετολμῆσθαι λεγομένοις ὑφ' Ἑλλήνων καὶ οὗτοι δράσαι παραδίδονται.* [Noah preached to them, but they would not listen so he fled the country.]

3) PG 6, 452.

4) ed. W. W. Harvey (Cambridge 1857) II, p. 279.

5) Eng. tr. (from Armenian) J. Smith, *St Irenaeus, Proof of the Apostolic Preaching* (Ancient Christian Writers 16), Westminster (Md.) London 1952.

6) ed. W. R. Schoedel (Oxford 1972), p. 60.

7) Clemens Alexandrinus II, p. 332 [GCS].

8) Pseudo-Klementinen I, pp. 126 f. [GCS].

represent it. All too may well have read ἄγγελοι in Genesis vi 2 as Eusebius *Preparatio Evangelica* V,4 certainly did [1]). Athenagoras and Justin turn to good account the references in Classical Mythology to unions of gods and humans and their offspring. The poets may have muddled the details or been deliberately misled by evil spirits, but they were on the right lines. The Homilist offers us the invaluable information that the giants were not the fabled monsters of Greek mythology but large men, bigger in body than men but smaller than angels. All these writers know the story-line of Enoch to which Tertullian explicitly refers. Tertullian alludes to Genesis vi 2 ff. several times. It is a useful text, explaining as it does the existence of idolatry and the difference between wives and women and offering a solemn warning against immodest feminine dress. In *De Virginibus Velandis* 7 [2]) he quotes Genesis vi 2 in the form *filii Dei* which he refers to angels along the lines of Enoch, a book possessed of divine authority; rejected it may be by the Jews for its references to Christ, but it has apostolic attestation from Jude and Enoch is indeed the most ancient prophet. The authority of Tertulian was sufficient to ensure that this interpretation has a following in the West. Cyprian [3]), Lactantius [4]), Ambrose [5]) and Commodian [6]) all in some measure represent it. Augustine mentions it respectfully only to reject it, it will be recalled.

In the East, though, voices were being raised against it in the first half of the 3rd century, as they were to be raised, until they became a clamour, against any notion of the pre-existence and descent of souls from the end of the 3rd century onwards. Julius Africanus in a fragment of his *Chronicle* [7]) cited by Syncellus alludes to Genesis vi 2. He quotes the text in the form ἄγγελοι but immediately goes on to remark that ἐν ἐνίοις ἀντιγράφοις εὗρον, οἱ υἱοὶ τοῦ θεοῦ and proceeds to interpret the phrase of Sethites whose intermarriage with Cainites angered God. If the text is applied to angels who revealed knowledge to their wives (a reference to Enoch vii 1) and produced children, it is incredible,

---

[1]) *Eusebius* VIII, 1, p. 229 [GCS].

[2]) Tertulliani Opera II, pp. 1216 f. [C Ch.2].

[3]) *De Hab. Virg.* 14 [CSEL 3, pp. 197 f. Microfiches Cards 3 f.].

[4]) *Instit.* II, 14 [CSEL 19, pp. 162 ff. Microfiches Card 3].

[5]) *De Noe et Arca* c. 4 [CSEL 32 i, p. 418. Microfiches Card 5]. The passage is heavily dependent on Philo, *Qu. and A. on Gen.*, I, 92 which it helps to explain.

[6]) *Instr.* I, 3 [CSEL 15, p. 7. Microfiches Card 1].

[7]) PG 10, 65.

he says, that God should have destroyed the whole race of men. Julius, taking a hint from Philo's third interpretation perhaps, thus rejects on grounds as obvious as they are reasonable both the reading ἄγγελοι and the intrepretation of Enoch, choosing instead an explanation wholly in terms of this world and its denizens.

To this kind of explanation and to this reading in the text the future belongs—at least for quite a long time. Why? The ground has in a sense been prepared by Philo. His first and third interpretations cut through what was felt, at least by the philosophically minded, to be absurd or superstitious. They raise doubts about taking the text at its face value, so to say, even if they do not succeed in resolving those doubts satisfactorily. Discard the connexion with the fall of souls, reject the authority of the book of Enoch and the way is open to a new view of the passage. Nonetheless, that view, I suggest, would not have come to dominate Christian exegesis, had it not been for 4th century debates about the deity of Christ. These debates were protracted and full of elements which do not presently concern us. It is enough to say that one point, the main point, at issue was whether the Son of God is eternally Son, Son by nature, and the Father eternally Father. An added impetus was thus given to exploring those texts of the Old Testament in which God is spoken of as, in some sense, Father and in which 'children' or 'sons' of God are named; other texts could be found, too, which appeared to designate human beings as God or gods. The principal texts here (though I have done no calculation to prove it) are: Isaiah i 2; Exodus iv 22; Psalm lxxxi (lxxxii) 1,6 [1]). Genesis vi 2 is not amongst the principal texts, nonetheless it could form a suitable appendage to them. It could prove against Marcellus as it does in Ps.-Athanasius *Contra Arianos* iv, 22 [2]), that the Word of God was Son before the Incarnation. Granted that the sonship of Christians is a derived sonship, that their right to address God as Father is a derived right, stemming from their relationship with Christ, then references to sons of God in the Old Testament (of which Genesis vi 2 is one) prove the reality of Christ's sonship before the Incarnation. Genesis vi 2 is thus accommodated within the Christian scheme of redemption and used to buttress it against one type of opponent.

---

1) Chrysostom *In Psalmum XLIX* [PG 55, 241 ff.] cites as examples of title 'God' applied to men: Ps. lxxxi (lxxxii) 1,6; Ex. xxii 28; Gen. vi 2; Lev. xxiv 15 f.; Jer. x 11; Gen. iv 26 [Enosh called 'God']; Ex. iv 22. All were by his time traditional 'places'.

2) ed. A. Stegmann (Tübingen 1917), p. 69.

Not that Genesis vi 2 often appears in the literature of the 4th century; it does not, and for the good reason that, as we saw at the hands of Julian, it may prove too much and in any case raise extraneous questions. It was never the main text on which a debate would hinge. But it could offer support for the main texts and supplement those passages in which, so Christain theologians thought, the Bible speaks of men as (καταχρηστικῶς) 'sons of God' or 'gods', by grace. By the time of Diodore [1] (and with him we begin a fresh set of debates about the humanity of Christ) that sense was probably well-established in the East, with the reading, of course, *υἱοὶ τοῦ θεοῦ*.

What about the West and the immediate sources for Augustine? Cyprian can refer to the story-line of Enoch, as the 'master', Tertullian, had done, and to much the same purpose. He interpreted the passage of unions between angels and human beings. The same is true of Lactantius and Commodian. Hilary disdains the use of Enoch to explain Psalm cxxxii (cxxxiii) 3 [2]. Hermon in Hebrew means 'anathema'. 'It is reported that there is a book by someone or other which says that the angels of God desiring the daughters of men congregated on this exceedingly high mountain when they came down from heaven. We will leave these things on one side; we ought not to acknowledge things not contained in the book of the law'. But Hilary does not apparently reject the notion of angelic unions. Neither does Ambrose, though he evidently has doubts. Something along the lines of Philo and pre-existent souls seems to be more to his taste. It was not to Jerome's taste. The descent of souls into bodies is manichaeism and manichaeism is what Origen's interpretation based on that apocryphal book (i.e. Enoch) amounts to [3]. The Hebrew word *Eloim* is either singular or plural. Aquila takes it in the plural, 'sons of gods', meaning by 'gods' either 'holy men' or 'angels'—compare Psalm lxxxi (lxxxii) 1. Symmachus has *filii potentium.* The book of Genesis has 'sons of God' not 'angels' [4]. It is these observations of Jerome, together with the

---

1) *Fragmenta in Genesim* (PG 33, 1570]. Diodore comments on Gen. vi 4. The giants are the long-lived men of renown of old, the sons of God who entered into the daughters of men. Their fault, punished by a reduction of life from 950 to 120 years, consisted in begetting sons not for God (so as to get their names from him or be called his sons) but for themselves.

2) *Tract. in Ps. cxxxii* c. 6 [CSEL 22, p. 689. Microfiches Card 7].

3) *Tract. de Ps. cxxxii* [C ch. 78, p. 280 f.].

4) *Hebr. Quaest. in Libro Genescos* [C ch. 72, p. 9 cf. p. 10]. cf. *Comm. in Esaiam* [C ch. 73A, p. 776].

tradition deriving from Tertullian, which influence the interpretation of Augustine and he is my terminus so far as the West is concerned.

As for Cyril's interpretation one puzzle remains to be resolved. Debates about the deity of Christ led, I suggested, to the connexion of Genesis vi 2 with other texts capable of proving the existence of 'sons of God' by grace in Old Testament times and hence the reality of the Word's true sonship prior to the Incarnation. Why did Cyril adopt the curious explanation that the "sons of God" of Genesis vi 2 are descendants of Enoch? Why did he not simply say that they were 'righteous' or 'holy'? It has nothing to do with Christological controversy and Cyril's rejection of the notion that the manhood of the Incarnate Son is a son of God by grace. Cyril has it in the *Glaphyra* (and so prior to the Nestorian controversy) and moreover it is Theodoret's explanation in *Questiones in Genesim* cap. VI [1]) as it was also Chrysostom's. This interpretation I have been unable to trace back further than Chrysostom [2]). It arises, of course, from taking Genesis iv 26 *ἐπικαλῖσεθαι* in the passive and the same ambiguity is inherent in Aquila's rendering *καλεῖσθαι*. Moreover, other passages in the Septuagint use the word in the sense of 'be called' [3]). The only explanation I have to offer (and it is a speculation based upon how the case might have been argued) is that Aquila's plural translation of האלהים confused the issue. 'Sons of (the) gods' implied natural descent in a way that 'sons of God' does not. If this speculation is sound and if the development of ideas I have sketched is plausible, the resulting interpretation is a curiously twisted skein, for the conclusion stands in marked contrast, indeed contradicts, the arguments by which it has been reached. Natural descent has been denied to make the *υἱοὶ τοῦ θεοῦ* sons of God 'by grace'. It is asserted to make them sons of Enosh. That this should be so will cause no surprise to historians of doctrine. The subject has skeins—indeed abounds in them—still more tangled than this.

---

1) PG 80, 148 ff.

2) It might, perhaps, have been Theodore's—see *In Ep ad Colossenses* [ed. H. B. SWETE, *Theodore of Mopsuestia on the minor epistles of St. Paul* I, p. 266 (Cambridge 1880)]: *nam et erant et alii ante Israel qui filiorum Dei nuncupatione digni fuerant habiti; de quibus Moyses dicit: videntes filii Dei* etc. Perhaps also Diodore's—*vide supra*. It is not implied for Gregory Nazianzen—see *Or*. 28, 18 (2nd Theological Oration) ed. J. BARBEL (Dusseldorf 1963), p. 98 and cf. *Carmina* 1,2,2 lines 490 ff. [PG 37, 617] where Gregory rejects the Philonic/Enochian explanation. Nor for Gregory of Nyssa—see *In Cant. Cant.* xv, ed. LANGERBECK (Leiden 1960), p. 453 :... *καὶ τῆς εἰς θεὸν ἐλπίδος τὸν 'Ενώς φησιν ἄρξασθαι.*

3) e.g. Gen. xlviii 16; Dt. xxviii 10.

REGISTER VAN BIJBELPLAATSEN

(Het register bevat enkel de belangrijkste Bijbelplaatsen, die in de voorafgaande opstellen aan de orde gesteld zijn)